THE COOKBOOK

THE

Vitality
COOKBOOK

Susan Clark

NEW MILLENNIUM BOOKS

VANCOUVER

Published in Canada in 1999 by
NEW MILLENNIUM BOOKS
8036 Enterprise Street, Burnaby
British Columbia V5A 1V7
Tel (604) 415-2444 Fax (604) 415-3444

Design copyright © The Ivy Press Limited 1999
Text copyright © Susan Clark 1999

Recipes devised by Erick Muzard

ISBN 1–894067–21–5

Note from the Publisher
Information given in this book is not intended to be
taken as a replacement for medical advice. Any person
with a condition requiring medical attention should
consult a qualified medical practitioner or therapist.

This book was conceived, designed, and produced by
THE IVY PRESS LIMITED
The Old Candlemakers
West Street
Lewes, East Sussex
BN7 2NZ

Creative Director: PETER BRIDGEWATER
Art Director: ALAN OSBAHR
Designer: BERNARD HIGTON
Editorial Director: DENNY HEMMING
Managing Editor: ANNE TOWNLEY
Project Editor: LORRAINE TURNER
Editor: NICOLA PRESTON
Illustrations: PIP ADAMS, JERRY FOWLER
Studio Photography: MARIE-LOU AVERY
Food Stylist: JACQUELINE CLARKE
Additional help with food styling: JOANNA FARROW,
FELICITY BARNUM-BOBB
Picture Research: LINDA MARSHALL

Reproduction and printing in Hong Kong by
HONG KONG GRAPHIC & PRINTING LTD

This book is typeset in Franklin Gothic and Bodoni

*For those who helped me hear the call back—especially
Nicola—and for my traveling companion, Declan*

The Publishers wish to thank the following for the use of
pictures:

A–Z Botanical Collection: p.20c.
Garden Picture Library: pp.18r, 158t.
Image Bank: pp.6l, 12c, 13c, 17l, 20l, 21t, 22cl, 22b, 22c,
24l, 26br, 27b, 28l, 160l, 168bl, 172r, 175t, 176b, 180l,
182l, 183b, 185t, 187br, 188b, 189t.
Science Photo Library: pp.14, 16c, 19cl, 24b, 158b, 161c,
168c, 181b, 184b.
Stock Market: pp.15t, 22l, 157bl, 174r, 177t.

contents

INTRODUCTION

We live in the Information Age and yet, in many ways, we have never been so ignorant about our health. Much of the traditional folklore that was used to prevent or fight disease long before the advent of modern drug-driven medicine has been lost or forgotten. Nobody has time to read food labels and, even if they do, some of the hidden ingredients, like the controversial genetically modified soy bean, have never been tested on humans anyway.

Biotechnology is the brave new science of the Millennium. Like the effect computers had on us at the end of the 20th century, it will radically change the way we all live and, especially, what we all eat. Yet even with these new products, we still don't really know what we are eating. Chemicals inevitably find their way into the food chain but current tests cannot even detect more than half of those known to be used in food production. There are no tests for what happens when these chemicals or other additives combine or when chemicals break down in the body and form new, usually dangerous, compounds called metabolites.

The biggest health risk we face every day is not getting behind the wheel of a car or boarding a transatlantic flight, but sitting down to a meal that has been so highly processed that all the nutritional value has been lost. What is left of the food is likely, in the long term, to make us sick.

Trying to be healthy has never been more difficult. Although we need to eat some fat to survive—including cholesterol, which is important for the manufacture of vitamin D and for the sheath membranes that protect nerves—a low-fat diet is healthier than a high-fat one. Yet many of the so-called low-fat products on the shelves are still high in fat and have been pumped full of sugar and additives to make them tastier and more appealing to a palate that is used to refined foods.

So which is riskier? The fat or the additives? Nobody has much time to cook anymore and even if you do produce a healthy, home-cooked meal, the kids will probably sulk and demand junk food. In fact, we're all so busy the food makers can get away with almost anything because nobody has time to worry about what they are eating.

The battle to better health is going to be a long one but it will be well worth the effort. The number of degenerative diseases is on the increase, with some experts predicting that by the year 2030 everyone will experience some form of cancer before death. We are all living longer and people who have worked hard all their lives want to be well enough to enjoy the fruits of their labors as they age.

You can take antiaging supplements that may help to swing the odds in your favor, but the one thing we know that works for sure is diet. The idea of using food as medicine is as old as Hippocrates—the Greek father of modern medicine who said "Let food be thy medicine." Hippocrates did not mean, of course, mass-produced hamburgers and french fries dripping in artery-blocking saturated fats. However, you can eat healthy versions of hamburgers—there's a recipe for them in the children's section of this book—but make them yourself so that you know exactly what you are eating.

Knowing what is on your plate is the key to this book and why you need to read it. Too often people take potluck with the most important thing in their lives—their health. You don't have to be a health freak, but it makes sense to look after the body which, if you nourish it properly, will serve you better than any machine you might buy.

To help you choose a healthy diet, and even to modify your diet to give you protection against, or help you recover from, specific ailments, we have devised over 100 recipes and then analyzed each one in detail for its nutritional benefits. Each recipe is also color-coded to show which conditions it can help you to fight. A meal that is bursting with the B vitamins and vitamin C, for instance, is a good stress-buster, while a dish

that is packed with potassium will help lower blood pressure, reduce allergies, and give you greater mental clarity because potassium sends oxygen to the brain.

Scientific research is beginning to prove the benefits of old-fashioned treatments. Your grandmother, for example, may have believed that the culinary herb sage was a "cure-all" and could help soothe an elderly and confused person. What she could not have known is that it does this by restoring impaired vascular supply to the brain. It is now believed that sage can play an important role in treating Alzheimer's disease. Sage is also excellent for helping the digestion.

We have used herbs in almost every dish, but if you wish to try sage in particular, you can substitute it for the lavender in our Summer Honey & Lavender Crème Brulée (*see page 112*). It may sound strange but it is delicious, and shows that herbs can cross the artificial boundary between savory and sweet dishes.

You will not find references to added salt in these recipes. When we say season to taste, we leave the option to salt or not to salt with you. Before you decide, however, remember that, while we need some salt in our diet in order to survive, we need less than 1 teaspoonful a day to stay healthy.

Sodium helps to maintain the acidity levels of the blood, keeps all the body's fluid levels healthy, and is important for healthy muscles. Too much sodium, however, can cause fluid to be retained by the tissues, which can lead to high blood pressure and a risk of heart disease. This in turn can aggravate existing conditions such as kidney disease, heart problems, and premenstrual disorder. The best advice is to be strict about limiting the amount of salt you use in your cooking and to avoid processed foods, which are almost always heavily salted.

Unless you buy organic produce, dairy foods can be contaminated by traces of hormones and antibiotics that are used in intensive farming to promote rapid growth and a bigger profit. To minimize the risk of eating chemicals that can upset the body's carefully balanced hormone levels and overburden the liver and digestive tract, we have suggested the use of substitute soy products in many of the recipes. When you buy these, make sure that they come from companies that do not use genetically modified soy beans; at least until someone does some testing on humans.

What this book does, like no other, is take all the guesswork out of what you are eating. No dish is in this book by accident. Every recipe has at least one and usually more nutritional benefits to commend it. Not only do we tell you, for example, that a dish is rich in vitamin A— an important antioxidant that is crucial for maintaining a healthy immune system and glowing skin—we also give you the precise percentage of the recommended daily allowance (RDA) for adults. In the children's meals, these figures reflect the percentage of a child's recommended daily allowance.

There is much dispute and debate about the RDAs because they are guidelines that show the minimum amount of a nutrient you need to avoid becoming ill through a deficiency. However, they fall far short of the doses that will promote optimum health.

These doses, often referred to as the Optimum Daily Allowance (ODA), are much higher but not yet agreed by the experts. In many of our recipes, the quantity of a vitamin or mineral supplied is much higher than the RDA. There is no risk of overload here—these dishes will help you to achieve optimum health and your body will flush out those nutrients it does not need.

Nowhere, in this book, will you find the word "calories" used in the context of losing weight. The best way to lose weight is to forget about dieting and adopt a healthy eating plan. When you switch to more wholesome, natural foods, you will automatically drop to the optimum weight for your build and stay there. You will feel better and your clothes will look better on you. You can eat as much of these foods as you want so there's no feeling of missing out. You'll also have twice, probably three times, the energy you had before.

Most of us ignore our health until we have a scare and can no longer take it for granted. If you are one of these people, you are very important because once you start to change your approach to your health and your diet, you can lead by example. You really can influence and change what the people you love are eating. And that's where a healthier lifestyle has to start—in your own home, in your own kitchen, with the people you care about.

As a health columnist for *The Sunday Times*, I know people are interested in their health and are eager to learn more. I get 100 letters every week from people all over the world who are frightened of a number of degenerative diseases and are trying to take responsibility for their own health. Many of these people know that diet can help but are not sure where to start. It is for these people that we have written this book. When I say we, I mean myself and the French chef, Erick

Muzard, who devised the recipes in this book. I deliberately wanted to work with a chef who adores food because, above all else, eating should be one of the greatest pleasures in your life. I also wanted to work with someone who did not have any built-in leanings toward healthy but boring eating plans, because I wanted recipes that look and taste delicious and that people cannot wait to cook. What I wanted, and what I think a lot of us want, is an enjoyable way of getting and staying healthy, as if almost by accident.

At the end of our work on these recipes, I asked Erick what health lesson, if any, he had learned from our research and our arguments (especially about butter and salt). He did not hesitate. "Eat more fresh fruits and vegetables," he said. "Buy organic produce. And, if like me you love the taste of meat and cannot give it up, make sure you know at least where it comes from and take steps to reduce the amount of saturated fat you're eating." I no longer eat meat, but I couldn't have put it better myself.

Happy healthy eating.

Section**One**

A DIET FOR LIFE

The only true cure for any condition is the body's inherent ability to heal itself. To do this it needs your help. The risk of developing diabetes, heart disease, cancer, and many other diseases that are linked to nutrition may be greatly reduced by improving your diet. By adapting the way you cook you can become your own healer.

Eating Well

There is no such thing as the "perfect" diet, but for decades now experts have agreed that there is a simple way of eating, based on nutritious wholegrains and seasonal fruits and vegetables, that will dramatically reduce the risk of disease. It is the kind of diet that used to get a bad press, but with degenerative diseases claiming millions of lives in the developed world, and with so many of us functioning well below par, it is the kind of diet that is finally getting the attention it deserves.

Put simply, people who eat a high-fiber, low-fat diet rich in raw fruits and vegetables and wholegrains will live longer than those who fail to wean themselves from the high-fat, low-fiber, sugar-laden diet that has become the norm in industrialized countries and which is responsible for so much illness.

If you want a long and healthy life, you should also make sure your diet is rich in the essential fatty acids that the body cannot make itself and cut back on sugar, protein, salt, caffeine, and alcohol.

FOOD FOR OPTIMUM HEALTH

Food is the source of energy for all physical and mental activity. Furthermore, the nutrients in the food we eat work together with our bodies to repair, maintain, and even replace every cell in the body about once every four months. As you read this, you are making over 200 million new cells to replace the same number of worn-out, dying cells, and you will continue to repeat this process every minute throughout your life.

The human body is the most magnificent example of evolution, still capable of blinding science with its sophistication and efficiency. But it can only function at optimum levels if you look after it. Feed it junk and bombard it with toxins and it will struggle to keep you healthy, but eventually will give up.

The good news is you don't have to be a health fanatic to give your body the best conditions for optimum health. During your lifetime food fads will come and go, but if you keep to the following guidelines, which can be modified when you have special nutritional needs, such as in pregnancy or when your immune system is under attack, you will be doing everything you can to remain healthy.

Eat a diet that is as natural as possible with plenty of unrefined seasonal nuts, fruits, and vegetables.

Wholegrains such as barley and rye are rich in protein and B vitamins.

BALANCED DIET

Wholegrains, such as corn, oats, barley, and rye, and fresh fruit and vegetables should form the basis of your diet. Aim to eat eight servings from these foods a day (a serving is equivalent to one slice of bread or half a bowl of rice; half a standard side salad, a broccoli floret, or a small apple).

Most of the animal protein you eat should come from cold-water fish, especially salmon, tuna, herring, and sardines, which contain essential fatty acids that help protect against cancers and heart disease. Eat oily fish at least three times a week. Eat meat sparingly—eat vegetarian sources of protein instead, such as nuts, seeds, and legumes, to help balance your diet.

Take your culinary inspiration from Nature.

When you eat dairy products, make sure they come from a good organic source and when you cook with oil, use cold-pressed, extra virgin olive oil.

Minimize the quantity of refined foods and sugar in your diet and try to avoid genetically modified foods and those that are pumped full of flavorings and additives. These have no nutritional value and may pose a threat to your health. Cut down, too, on stimulants like alcohol and caffeine, which tax the liver, affecting its ability to purify the blood and eliminate toxins.

Finally, you need plenty of uncontaminated, pure water to help your body flush out harmful toxins, so drink eight glasses of water a day. Drinking water before or after (but not during) a meal also helps to digest food properly.

ORGANIC, SEASONAL PRODUCE

We are the first generation whose bodies have had to cope with food grown in soil depleted of nutrients and an onslaught of toxins from the environment and from chemically processed food. Whenever possible it is best to eat organically grown foods because they contain more nutrients than highly processed foods and will be free of the pesticides, herbicides, chemical fertilizers, hormones, and antibiotics that are used in intensive farming.

As well as eating food that has been produced organically, take your inspiration from the seasons. Throughout this book the emphasis is on fresh foods, because it makes sense to eat produce that has been grown locally and is in season. In the winter, cook warming, nourishing dishes containing nutrient-rich nuts, root vegetables, and tubers, such as potatoes. In the spring, which is a time of new growth and rapid expansion, eat energy-rich fruits and serve dishes piled high with delicious new shoots and vitamin-rich young greens.

REGULAR MEALS

Skipping meals sends the body into starvation mode encouraging it to stockpile fat reserves. It also results in mood swings. You should eat a moderate-sized breakfast, a large lunch, and a moderate-sized evening meal. Keeping to regular eating habits will give you energy all day and will regulate digestion and sleep patterns. If you do need to snack, eat fruit, or nuts and seeds.

HEALTHY PREPARATION

Your body requires over 70 nutrients to function at its best and eating a variety of whole, fresh foods that have been tampered with as little as possible after harvesting will help provide many of these. Cooking can destroy some of these nutrients, so try to include some raw foods, such as a side salad, in your diet every day. When you do cook, use gentle methods. Steaming, for instance, is less aggressive than boiling, preserving more of the vitamins and minerals in foods, and baking is better than frying.

10
point plan to improve your diet

1 Eat at least 3–5 servings of fruit and vegetables each day

2 Drink at least 8 glasses of water each day

3 Limit the amount of alcohol you drink (see page 25)

4 Drink no more than 5 cups of tea, coffee, or soda daily

5 Eat a healthy breakfast

6 Eat fish at least three times per week

7 Eat no more than 2 portions of red meat each week

8 Cut down on ready-prepared foods you eat

9 Replace butter and animal fat with vegetable oil where possible

10 Do not add extra salt to food

Food
Groups

To maintain your health and fight off disease you need a balanced diet that includes all of the five main nutrient groups in the correct proportions and plenty of pure water. The five groups are carbohydrates, proteins, fats, vitamins, and minerals. A diet based on nourishing wholegrains and fruit and vegetables with small amounts of fish, dairy products, and meat will meet all your dietary needs and keep you in good health.

Starch molecules seen through a microscope.

CARBOHYDRATES

ALL SUGARS AND STARCHES INCLUDING THOSE FOUND IN BREAD, PASTA, RICE, CEREAL GRAINS, LEGUMES, FRUITS, VEGETABLES, TABLE SUGAR, HONEY, SYRUP, SUGARY FOODS

Made up of carbon, hydrogen, and oxygen, carbohydrates produce energy when the carbon molecules bind with oxygen in the bloodstream. It's best to eat complex carbohydrates such as bread and pasta, in preference to sugar—the other type of carbohydrate. Too high an intake of sugary foods such as desserts, cakes, chocolate, candies, and sodas, increases your risk of obesity, diabetes, and heart disease. Complex carbohydrates are the best source of energy (glucose) that fuels all the body's functions. They have a more complicated molecular structure than simple sugars, which means they are broken down more slowly, releasing a steady flow of energy into the bloodstream. They help with the digestion and absorption of other foods, including protein and fat metabolism. Carbohydrates can prevent constipation, reduce the risk of cancer of the colon, and regulate cholesterol levels.

Meat is composed of strands of fiber.

PROTEIN

MEAT, POULTRY, FISH, EGGS, MILK AND MILK PRODUCTS, WHOLEGRAINS, SOY AND SOY PRODUCTS, LEGUMES, NUTS, CEREAL GRAINS

Essential for growth and development, protein also provides energy. It is needed to make hormones, enzymes, antibodies, and healthy tissues and to regulate the acid/alkali balance of the body. Protein is composed of about 20 amino acids, of which eight, known as "essential" amino acids, must come from food (the body can synthesize the rest). Essential amino acids are provided by "complete" proteins such as meat, fish, poultry, eggs, cheese, and soy. "Incomplete" proteins, which include those from grains, legumes, and leafy green vegetables, provide only some of the essential amino acids and therefore need to be eaten in combination (a Mexican wheat tortilla with refried beans, for example) if the body is to obtain all the building blocks it needs to construct protein. Meat and dairy products do contain complete protein, but eat them sparingly because they are high in fat.

The fat globules in milk are clearly visible in this view.

FATS

MONOUNSATURATED FATS, FOUND IN VEGETABLE AND NUT OILS SUCH AS OLIVE AND PEANUT OIL; POLYUNSATURATED FATS, INCLUDING SUNFLOWER AND SOY OILS, OILY FISH, WALNUTS, AND WHEAT GERM; SATURATED FATS, FOUND IN MEAT AND DAIRY PRODUCTS

The food industry promotes low-fat food heavily because consumers are willing to pay more for such products (many of which are full of sugar and additives). Even so, the rate of obesity continues to climb. It has doubled in the last decade and the problem is now so bad that the World Health Organization (WHO) has declared it an epidemic. Fat, the most concentrated source of energy, is needed by the body and not all fats are bad. For example, essential fatty acids promote good health. What we do not need, however, are large quantities of the wrong kind. Excess fat can also lead to high blood pressure, heart disease, and cancer of the colon.

All fats are made up of fatty acids and are categorized according to the number of hydrogen atoms in the acids. Saturated fatty acids are the bad guys because they raise blood cholesterol levels. The US National Cholesterol Education Program recommends that saturated fats should make up no more than 10 percent of your daily calorie intake. If you have heart or circulatory problems, even that is far too high.

Polyunsaturated fats are good for you, lowering overall cholesterol levels. However, they reduce the good type of cholesterol, which protects against heart disease, as well as the bad type that increases the risk. Monounsaturated fats, however, appear to lower bad cholesterol levels without reducing the amount of good cholesterol.

When polyunsaturated oils are altered through hydrogenation, the industrial process used in making margarine and other products, they form "trans-fats." Avoid products with these; studies have found they help raise cholesterol levels.

Drink plenty of pure water.

WATER

Essential to life, water is involved in almost every function of the body. It transports nutrients to and from the cells and is crucial for all circulatory, digestive, and excretory functions. Water is also necessary for regulating the body's temperature. Few people drink enough water, and the biggest (and least expensive) favor you can do for your health is to drink eight glasses a day. Your skin will glow and you will see for yourself how it plays such a pivotal role in good health.

For optimum health, nutritionists recommend drinking steam-distilled water whenever you can. The distillation process eliminates bacteria, viruses, chemicals, and other pollutants. If you suffer from digestive disorders, avoid carbonated bottled water because it can irritate the intestines.

FOR GUIDANCE ON THE REMAINING NUTRIENT GROUPS, VITAMINS AND MINERALS, SEE PAGES 16–17.

A Good Diet?

Your idea of a "healthy" diet may not be accurate. Compare the following:

Day 1
BREAKFAST
Grapefruit, orange juice, toast, reduced fat spread

LUNCH
Cottage cheese, large mixed salad, piece of fruit

DINNER
Skinned, broiled chicken, large salad, fruit salad

Day 2
BREAKFAST
Baked beans on wholemeal toast. Toast with scraping of butter and honey

LUNCH
Tuna fish and scallion sandwich, red-and-green pepper salad

DINNER
Vegetable soup, broiled chicken, potatoes, green vegetables, slice of Brie and wholemeal bread

Day 1 is missing essential calcium, protein, zinc, selenium, potassium, and fiber; but Day 2 is healthy and balanced to ensure that you get protein, carbohydrate, fat, and fiber.

1 Green vegetables
2 Legumes
3 Fruit
4 Meat
5 Dairy products
6 Potatoes
7 Fish

Vitamins and Minerals

Vitamins and minerals are necessary for a whole range of body functions, yet they are frequently missing from the diet. You can eat all the right foods in the right proportions but there is still no guarantee that you will be getting all the nutrients you need. It is also impossible to harvest foods that are rich in vitamins and minerals from soil that has been stripped of all its goodness by intensive farming. You might therefore wish to consider taking supplements.

Manufacturing and refining techniques rob food of much of its nutritional value, while packaging processes, additives, pesticides, and artificial preservatives—all designed to give food a longer shelf life and a more appetizing look— replace nutrients with questionable chemicals. Switching to an organic, chemical-free diet wherever possible is the single most important step you can take toward reclaiming your health.

In an ideal world, you would get all the nutrients you need from your healthy, organic diet, but for most of us, the demands of a busy life make this almost impossible, however good our intentions. Entire families exist almost exclusively on convenience foods, and even the most dedicated disciples of healthy eating cannot always make sure every meal is properly balanced.

This means that supplementing your diet with vitamins and minerals is the next best method of staying well throughout your life. Supplements are no substitute for healthy, wholesome foods and you cannot use them to try to counter too many fast-food takeouts, but they are a useful adjunct to a nutrient-rich diet.

Chemical Bread
Consider this: a hundred years ago, a loaf of bread contained just five natural ingredients, which provided around 24 wholesome nutrients. Today, a commercial loaf is often an unsavory cocktail of 100 constituents, including residues of chemicals from the packaging, preservatives, colorings, and fungicides. Some may have three or four of the nutrients stripped out and then replaced, so the bread can be sold as "enriched" with fortifying vitamins.

Close-up view of the mitochondria that oxidize fats and sugars to provide energy for body cells.

Do Your Homework
In the US the complementary health market is estimated to be worth as much as $27 billion and in the UK people spend £360 million a year on nutritional and herbal supplements. There is a staggeringly confusing array of supplements on offer and I suspect many manufacturers are only too happy to blind us with jargon and pseudo-science. Supplements themselves go in and out of fashion, and many of us are further confused by terms like supernutrients and megavitamins. (The latter is used to describe very high doses of vitamins, which are prescribed to try to reverse an existing condition.) Supplements are expensive and I am always shocked by the way people take them randomly. You wouldn't hazard a guess that the car needed an oil change, would you? So why take a stab in the dark with something as important as your health?

Even though we all need the same nutrients, the quantity we require will differ according to our age, lifestyle, body weight, gender, and levels of exercise. There is only one way to find out what you should be taking and that is to have a test.

Brown bread made with unrefined flour is more nutritious than white bread.

Supplements for Life

Vitamin A: Helps all cells reproduce normally and maintains healthy membranes and skin, which prevent microorganisms that cause disease from entering. Found naturally in green leafy vegetables, liver, dairy products, and cod liver oil.

Vitamin E: Protects against heart disease and enhances the activity of vitamin A. A powerful antioxidant, it can slow down aging and protect against blood clots. Found in wheat-germ oil, nuts, seeds, vegetable oils, egg yolks, and leafy greens.

Vitamin C: Another potent antioxidant that mops up the cancer-causing free radicals, which also cause premature aging. Promotes wound-healing and fights viruses. Broccoli and citrus fruits are good food sources.

Selenium: Activates an antioxidant enzyme called glutathione peroxidase, which may protect against cancer. Also regulates the thyroid hormones and protects against clogging of the arteries. Best sources are brazil nuts, organic bread, and seafood.

Zinc: Essential for the synthesis of DNA, it is also a constituent of more than 300 enzymes involved in tissue repair, digestion, fertility, vision, cell reproduction, and protein synthesis. Fights disease by bolstering the immune system. Foods rich in zinc include pumpkin seeds, tofu, eggs, oysters, and other seafood.

Coenzyme Q10: Found in the mitochondria (where energy is generated) in almost every cell and in highest concentrations in the heart and the liver. It can strengthen muscle and protects against heart disease and diabetes. Natural sources are spinach, broccoli, nuts, meat, and fish.

Folic acid (Vitamin B$_8$): Lowers levels of homocysteine: a by-product of metabolism now accepted as a more accurate indicator of the risk of heart disease than cholesterol levels. Also prevents birth defects. Found in beans, meat, and leafy greens.

Manganese: Needed for healthy skin, bone and cartilage formation, and crucial in protecting against osteoporosis. Too much calcium, iron, and zinc will reduce its absorption. Good sources include nuts, seeds, pineapple, wheat bran, and greens.

Magnesium: More people are deficient in this mineral than any other. Crucial for the formation of new cells, bone, protein, and fatty acids, it also activates the stress-busting B vitamins, regulates energy production, and controls insulin levels. Food sources include nuts and grains, fish, meat, and leafy vegetables.

Probiotics: Dysbiosis ("leaky gut" caused by imbalance in the colon bacteria) can lead to pervasive yeast infections, lowered resistance to disease, and irritable bowel syndrome. Probiotics help rebalance the gut flora. They are found in natural yoghurt.

Fish oils: These omega-3-rich oils contain compounds the body cannot make itself. They have anti-inflammatory properties and also regulate blood triglyceride levels to protect against heart disease. Good food sources include oily fish, especially mackerel, salmon, herring, sardines, and anchovies.

A simple sweatpatch test, arranged by a qualified health practitioner, will take the guesswork out of supplementing your diet and will save you a small fortune in the long run.

ANTIOXIDANTS

Many vitamins and minerals have potent anti-cancer and antiaging antioxidant properties. Antioxidant means the supplement can "mop up" the free radical molecules that are a normal by-product of metabolism and which, if left to scavenge in the body, can cause cell damage.

SYNERGY

While each vitamin and mineral has a specific function in the body, they are all interrelated and work together (nutritionists call this synergy). So changing your intake of one can, inadvertently, affect your absorption of another. Too much calcium, for example, can cause a deficiency in zinc, iron, magnesium, and phosphorous by preventing their absorption in the body. This means that it is important to visit a nutritionist for a tailor-made list of supplements, rather than taking potluck.

Supplements can enhance the action of an organic diet rich in oily fish, citrus fruits, garlic, and green leafy vegetables.

Herbsand **Spices**

Herbs and spices don't just add flavor and interest to a dish—they can bring numerous health benefits, too. Ginger may help protect against heart disease, licorice soothes digestive disorders, and cilantro helps detoxify an overburdened liver. Try to use fresh herbs whenever you can. The easiest way to have herbs on hand is to grow your own. Many herbs are easy to cultivate at home. You can then enjoy their revitalizing aroma in cooking and also every time you brush by.

If you cook regularly, the chances are you will already have a bountiful medicine chest in your kitchen store cupboard. Did you know, for example, that in India's traditional Ayurvedic medicine, basil is used to treat stomach, kidney, and blood ailments or that cooking with cumin will help boost your body's ability to absorb other important nutrients? Spices can enhance health and self-healing too. Just one teaspoon (5g) of ground cinnamon, for instance, provides 61mg of bone-building calcium, 25mg of potassium, 1.43mg of vitamin C, and traces of the antioxidant vitamin A.

Cultivate your own herb garden to provide a supply of healing natural medicines all year long.

Herbal Teas

Herbal medicine is completely natural and works by treating the cause of ill health, rather than the symptoms. You will benefit from herbs' healing power if you use them to flavor food, but if you want to use them properly as medicines to treat disease, you should drink them in a tea. Simply add a large teaspoon of powdered herb to a cup and pour on boiling water. Infuse for 10 minutes and drink while hot. (Sweeten with honey if you like.)

WHAT IS AN HERB?

An herb is any plant that is valued for its medicinal, culinary, or aromatic qualities. As well as livening up a dull recipe, herbs can be used to relax, soothe, and energize, as well as to target specific organs, fight infection, bolster natural defenses against disease, and ease aches and pains.

Herbs can also be effective where conventional medicines are impotent. Antibiotics, for example, cannot eliminate viral infections, but many herbs can.

Herbal remedies are powerful and they make up three-quarters of all the medicines used in the world. Indeed, the very word "drug" comes from the early German word *droge*, meaning to dry, as in drying herbs. It is estimated that up to half of all prescription drugs either come directly from plants or are chemical imitations of constituents found naturally in plants. Aspirin, for example, now considered a cure for conditions as diverse as heart disease and cataracts, is, in fact, a chemical imitation of salicin, an acid derived from the bark of the white willow tree. Even less exotic herbs like parsley have an important role in promoting optimum health. This herb, which you can chew to freshen the breath after eating garlic, can aid digestion and clear congestion caused by coughs and colds.

NEW WAYS OF USING OLD FAVORITES

The use of plants for healing goes back to prehistoric times. Our ancestors worked intuitively with herbs, which they harvested themselves. Today, new research has thrown light on extraordinary properties of many everyday plants. Rosemary, for example, is a powerful antioxidant and has been shown to strengthen heartbeat. Sage, which has impressive antiaging properties, can restore impaired vascular supply to the brain and may play a role in treating Alzheimer's disease. While such herbs are anything but new, Western herbalists are changing the way they use them. The old idea that only one herb should be used to treat a particular condition has been usurped by polypharmacy, or the practice of treatments based on combinations of different herbs.

THE WONDER HERBS

The idea of a "new herb" is a contradiction in terms because healing plants that have only recently become popular in the West have been in existence for thousands of years and used by traditional cultures throughout that time. Echinacea (pronounced Ek-in-ay-she-ah) is a good example. Now one of the best-selling herbal remedies on both sides of the Atlantic, it was first used by the Native American Sioux for snake bites and healing wounds. A potent immune-booster, this antibacterial and antiviral herb can also ease psoriasis and eczema.

Staphylococcus aureus, a common bacterium, is kept in check by herbs such as garlic.

Also new to the West are the powerful immune-boosting medicinal mushrooms, shiitake, reishi, and maiitake. The latter, which grows to the size of a basketball and is known as the dancing mushroom, is being marketed as a treatment for yeast infections. Shiitake is used as a cancer-fighting agent in China and Japan (try Shiitake Soup, see page 36), and reishi is used to prevent heart disease.

Remember, although culinary quantities of herbs are safe, herbal remedies, like any medicines, can be very potent and should be handled with care. In particular, if you are pregnant, breastfeeding, or taking medication, see your doctor or a qualified medical herbalist first.

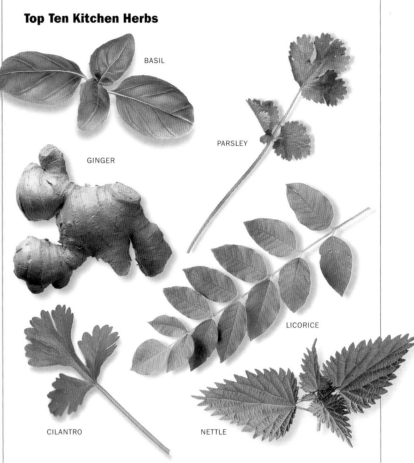

Top Ten Kitchen Herbs

BASIL

PARSLEY

GINGER

LICORICE

CILANTRO

NETTLE

ROSEMARY

GARLIC

Ginger: A spiritual and physical cleanser, good for coughs, colds, indigestion, motion sickness, morning sickness, arthritis, and circulatory problems.

Basil: Stimulates the immune system to make more antibodies. Relieves many conditions, including asthma, arthritis, rheumatism, and headaches.

Rosemary: A gentle liver tonic, it stimulates circulation, strengthens the heartbeat, and is a good antidote to stress.

Sage: Astringent and antiseptic, it has powerful antiaging properties, enhances memory, and may help protect against Alzheimer's disease.

Cilantro: Antifungal and antibacterial action aids digestion and alleviates allergies and hayfever. Decongests the liver and eases cystitis and skin rashes.

Turmeric: May aid fat loss and boosts circulation. Energizes the immune system and speeds up wound healing.

Fenugreek: Relieves constipation, lowers cholesterol, and reduces blood-sugar levels. Soothes coughs, fevers, sore throats, and menstrual pain.

Nettle: Protects against anemia, allergies and hayfever, high blood pressure, and heart disease. Can also alleviate the symptoms of prostate enlargement.

Garlic: Potent antibacterial agent, effective against colds, skin problems, and digestive disorders. Can also help circulatory disorders.

Licorice: Alleviates stomach disorders, bronchitis, sore throats, coughs, kidney problems, and irritable bowel syndrome (IBS).

Food Safety

You may think that you know what's on your plate but it's likely that you never have time to read the food labels on jars or ready-cooked meals, and even if you do, would you recognize what all those long chemical names really mean? They say that ignorance is bliss, but when it comes to the food you eat, it's downright dangerous. The more you know about how food is grown, prepared, processed, packaged, and colored, the more you will be able to protect your own and your family's health.

Flamingo feathers and beetles are just some of the unsavory ingredients that can end up in our food.

What do a Mexican cactus beetle, a flamingo feather, and a burned vegetable have in common? They are all used to produce food colorings, which are then said to have come from "natural" sources. The beetle is crushed and the carcass used to make cochineal (E120), which has been linked with food intolerances, the flamingo feathers produce canthaxanthin (E161), now banned in food but still allowed in chicken feed to color egg yolks, and those charred vegetables produce an additive called carbon black, which is as unappetizing as it sounds.

Look Before You Eat

Many of the additives in current use are simply presumed safe. Others have been deemed safe, but are already suspected of causing problems. Others are still in the throes of being tested. If you, or any member of your family, suffer from asthma, hyperactivity, aspirin sensitivity, phenylketonuria, or gout, you should avoid food additives, colorings, and preservatives, and consult a nutritionist.

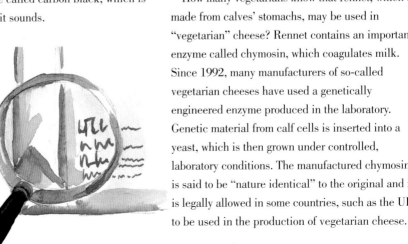

Since 1940, when the per capita intake of chemical additives and preservatives was first recorded, the quantity of artificial colorings added to the diet in the US has rocketed by 995 percent. How do you know, for instance, that the loaf of "healthy" brown bread from the supermarket is not simply white bread dyed with caramel coloring? The answer is you don't.

AN ADDITIVE BY ANY OTHER NAME?

Most additives have to be declared, but there are several thousand flavoring additives that do not have an E number and do not have to be listed. Manufacturers know that consumers have become ultrawary of anything that contains E numbers and so many fudge the issue by avoiding the use of numbers altogether. Instead, they give the ingredient its full chemical name and hope we are all too busy to read the label, let alone find out what that chemical is. Food processing aids, including the solvents and propellants that are used to carry additives into food, do not have to be declared, even though traces of these may find their way into the finished product.

How many vegetarians know that rennet, which is made from calves' stomachs, may be used in "vegetarian" cheese? Rennet contains an important enzyme called chymosin, which coagulates milk. Since 1992, many manufacturers of so-called vegetarian cheeses have used a genetically engineered enzyme produced in the laboratory. Genetic material from calf cells is inserted into a yeast, which is then grown under controlled, laboratory conditions. The manufactured chymosin is said to be "nature identical" to the original and it is legally allowed in some countries, such as the UK, to be used in the production of vegetarian cheese.

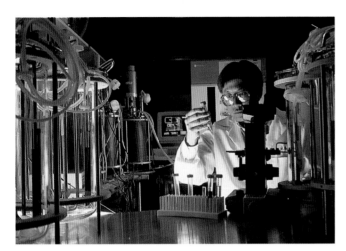

High-tech laboratory techniques allow scientists to grow animal cells for use in food manufacture.

FRANKENSTEIN FOOD

Most consumers do not like the idea of genetically engineered or irradiated foods. Such foods are very common in the food industry, for example soy and soy oil are constituents of over 7,000 everyday foods, so it is hard to avoid eating the controversial, genetically engineered version. (There is, to date, no evidence that modified soy is harmful to humans, although its effects on people have not been tested.)

The idea of irradiation to prolong shelf life has proved to be very unpopular in some countries. For example, in the UK, despite the fact that the UK government made it legal in 1991, only one British company has a license to do it, and then only on herbs and spices. Sue Dibb, codirector of The Food Commission (an independent organization in the UK that lobbies for the consumer to be told the truth about food), is the author of a book entitled *What The Label Doesn't Tell You*, which warns that thousands of tons of food are irradiated each year and nobody will say where they end up. (Processed and restaurant foods are the obvious suspects in this case.) If you read that book, supermarket shopping will never be the same.

The notion that bombarding food with gamma rays (irradiation) would make the food radioactive and toxic to consumers caused a big food scare in Europe. These fears proved to be unfounded. However, there are hidden dangers as highlighted, for example, by the case of a cargo of irradiated and lethal shrimp shipped to Europe from the Far East. The shrimp had been contaminated with cholera and, after tests, scientists found that while this process had indeed killed the bacteria, it had not destroyed the toxins they produce.

By law, any food or ingredient that has been irradiated must say so, except if it makes up less than 25 percent of a compound ingredient. So food that may look fresh may be stale and stripped of most of its vitamins.

In the US, fruit that has been waxed or sprayed with insecticide must say so. In the UK, you had better peel that shiny red apple, because it is probably covered in shellac, or E904—an insect secretion—also used to glaze candies and cake decorations. Or you could give it to your least favorite person!

Don't judge by appearances: healthy-looking apples, eggs, and bread may all contain gruesome food additives.

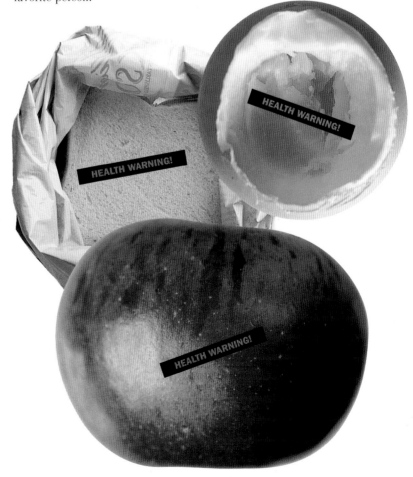

Fast Food

With fast-food outlets on every corner, if you want to stay healthy it is important to wise up to their dangers. Of course you can enjoy the occasional takeout with family and friends, but on the whole this type of food tends to be laden with sugar, fat, and flavor enhancers, such as monosodium glutamate. It makes sense to be careful about what you order. More rice and less korma may sound depressing, but if you persevere, you'll soon find that you have retrained your tastebuds.

Fast-paced modern living dictates that we eat more and more food from takeout joints.

Barnstaple is a small, rural market town on the glorious North Devon coast of England. Once, there were no sinful fast-food outlets to lead you astray, unless you count those good old British institutions selling cholesterol-laden fish and chips and worse – the kind of heart-attack-in-a-bag, grease-sodden street food that sends any nutritionist worth their salt into paroxysms of dire health warnings, but which remains so beloved of Britons everywhere.

I know this because I grew up here and, as a child, looked forward to the occasional treat of crispy battered cod and soggy chips. Today, children living in Barnstaple can persuade mom and dad to visit any one of 45 fast-food outlets, ranging from Italian to Indian. And, of course, there's McDonalds.

When I was growing up it didn't matter much if we sometimes ate what would now be called junk food, because the rest of our diet was so nutritious. Homegrown vegetables came from the garden, complete with mud and slugs. We were organic long before anyone talked about being organic, and we ate what was in season because that's all that was available—we didn't know anything different.

The picture is very different now. All over the world, fast food has become the mainstay of many families' diets. In one recent survey, a third of nutritionists questioned owned up to succumbing to a hamburger, pizza, Chinese, Mexican, or Indian meal at least once a week. We eat, on average, an estimated 9lb (4kg) of potato chip-type snacks per person every year and what is clear is that fast food is here to stay.

MAKING SENSIBLE CHOICES

Unlike supermarkets, takeout restaurants have no legal obligation to tell you what's in the food that they stuff between tacos, pile high onto limp sesame buns, or cram into crispy pitta bread. So, it's up to you to monitor what you eat and choose the healthiest options. I give you plenty of tips on how to do this on the next page.

As long as the rest of your diet is healthy and you exercise, there's no reason why you can't enjoy fast food from time to time. It's junk *diets*, not junk *foods* we need to worry about, and for those eating balanced and healthy meals most of the time, the odd hamburger, pizza, taco, or fish and chips is not going to prove a fast track to the city morgue.

With fast-food takeouts everywhere offering cheap, mouthwatering, fat-laden food, is it any wonder that obesity is reaching epidemic proportions?

Top Ten Tips for a Healthier Takeout

1 The single most important health tip to reduce the number of empty calories and unhealthy saturated fats in your takeout food, is to order more of the more nutritious, carbohydrate dishes, such as rice, and to opt for steamed or lightly stir-fried vegetables instead of deep-fried fatty foods.

2 The first pizzeria opened its doors in New York in 1895 and pizzas are still the fastest-growing sector of the fast food industry. Make yours healthier by ordering regular crust (thin and deep pan are both higher in fat), going easy on the cheese, and topping it with healthy vegetables.

3 Classic Chinese cooking is very healthy, but most takeaway joints corrupt these dishes to make them appealing to the Western palate. Watch out for and avoid dishes laden with animal fat, liberal sprinklings of sugar, and monosodium glutamate (MSG).

4 Filling up on plain, boiled rice and noodles will greatly improve the nutritional value of your Chinese takeout. Avoid the egg-fried "special" versions, which can contain lots of unhealthy cholesterol-raising fat, sugar, and empty calories. For your main dish, order steamed or stir-fried vegetables and chicken or shrimp, which are lower in fat than beef, lamb, or duck.

5 Avoid that old favorite—sweet and sour. Independent analysis by The UK Food Commission found a portion of sweet and sour chicken with egg-fried rice totaled 2,025 calories; almost ¼lb (100g) of fat plus generous dollops of sugar and salt.

6 Follow similar guidelines with Indian food: fill up on the bulky carbohydrate dishes. Instead of fatty naan breads, order dry-fried chapatis, which also contain valuable B vitamins and fiber.

7 Cream-based kormas and deep-fried bhajis may be delicious, but they are high in empty calories and unhealthy fat. Choose the dry-fried dishes instead.

8 If you must eat fish and chips, find a place that cooks with sunflower or other oils that are low in saturated fats. Avoid those that use a saturated vegetable fat, such as palm oil, animal shortening fat, or beef dripping. Ask for a small portion of chips and fill up later with a slice of whole-wheat bread once you get home.

9 Hamburgers get bad press, but you can make your meal healthier by leaving out the cheese, which is probably processed and full of additives and colorings. A good quality hamburger is reasonably healthy: it provides protein, iron, zinc, and vitamin B_{12}. It is high in fat but it is a healthier choice than fried chicken. Steer clear of cheap hamburgers, which are loaded with added fats and unsavory E numbers.

10 Make eating a hamburger healthier by saying no to the chips. Sadly, those thin french fries, often flavored with saturated animal fats, are the worst kind because proportionately there's less potato and more fat in them than thick-cut chips.

Stir-fried Chinese food is one of the healthiest takeouts.

Mono-unsaturated sunflower oil reduces cholesterol.

A hamburger made from lean meat with lots of salad is a healthy choice.

Pitta and falafel with plenty of salad is a good choice (but skip the mayonnaise).

Chunky french fries contain far less fat than their thin cousins.

Safe Drinking

Drinking may be pleasurable, but the health benefits are minimal and the risks are enormous. Drinking alcohol in moderation can have physical and psychological benefits—but the key word is moderation. Alcohol is a stimulant. It causes health problems on its own account and also exacerbates numerous degenerative diseases. Safe drinking guidelines vary from individual to individual, but stick to one drink a day if you're female and less than three if you're male.

A drink or two a day with friends is one of life's pleasures, but it's important to stay within the recommended limits.

Guess the nationality of the researcher who won worldwide plaudits when he published research suggesting that drinking red wine will protect you from cancer, as well as from heart disease? He was French, of course.

I say "of course" because Serge Renaud, a researcher at the University of Bordeaux, is probably one of those Frenchmen enjoying what the rest of the world calls The French Paradox. It is a question that has taxed the best brains in the field of nutrition for years and which continues to divide experts.

How can the French, whose diet is notoriously high in saturated animal fats, rank only 17th in the world's league table of heart disease? Some researchers have suggested that the answer lies at the bottom of a bottle of red wine. They believe that phenolic flavonoids, nonalcoholic substances found in grape skins, can prevent the build-up of LDL or "bad" cholesterol and plaque in the arteries, which can lead to a stroke or coronary heart disease. The reason red wine and not white wine is said to confer benefits is that red wines are made by fermenting grapes with their skins on. More recent research has questioned the verity of health claims made about red wine, with some scientists suggesting that many grape varieties lose their antioxidant potency with age. One study published by the Rowett Research Institute in Aberdeen suggested the antioxidant properties of a 12-year-old malt whisky last longer in the body than those of red wine.

RAISE A GLASS TO OLD AGE

A larger survey has confirmed what many studies have shown, that alcohol, in moderation, can help to lower the risk of fatal heart disease. This research, conducted by The American Cancer Society over a nine-year period, was originally initiated to monitor the effects of alcohol in relation to cancer, and documented the impact of a drink a day on almost half a million men and women aged between 30 and 104, whose average age at the start of the survey was 56.

It showed that it is in middle age when alcohol's contribution to a healthy heart is expected to pay off, outweighing concerns about its ill-effects, which include a slightly increased risk of cancer.

Drinking alcohol in moderation has been shown to have both physical and psychological benefits. It can help to reduce stress, decrease tension and anxiety, and encourage more relaxed, pleasant feelings of sociability and unself-

Plaque (colored yellow) can build up in the arteries due to too much "bad" cholesterol in the blood. Substances in red wine may help prevent the build-up.

consciousness. In the elderly, alcohol has a range of benefits: it has been shown to stimulate a healthier appetite, promote regular bowel function, and improve overall mood.

SENSIBLE DRINKING LIMITS

The subject of sensible drinking remains confusing, not least because people are still not clear what constitutes a "unit."

The American Department of Health and Human Services, for example, which probably has the strictest criteria, defines "moderate drinking" as no more than two drinks a day for men and one for women. A standard drink is deemed to be 12fl oz (350ml) beer, 5fl oz (150ml) of wine or 1½fl oz (30ml) of 80-proof distilled spirits. Each of these drinks contains roughly the same amount (½fl oz/15ml) of alcohol.

Safe drinking guidelines vary wildly between countries, and in any case, the same amount of alcohol can affect two people very differently. In the UK, for example, the guidelines are more generous but still fall way behind other European countries, especially France. British men are advised to stick to 3–4 units a day, while women are restricted to 2–3. One unit equates to ⅓fl oz/10ml of alcohol. To many British people, drinking a bottle of wine (six UK units) sounds much worse than drinking three pints of beer (also six units, since half a pint of beer is one unit).

Research has shown that, given the same amount of alcohol, women become more intoxicated than men. For this, blame biology. There is an enzyme that works in the stomach tissue to break down alcohol before it reaches the bloodstream. This enzyme is four times more active in men than it is in women. Also, women have, proportionately, more body fat and less body fluid than men. Because alcohol is more soluble in water than in fat, the same dose becomes more concentrated in the body of a woman than in the body of a man.

Based on research that shows that those with the lowest rates of mortality were men who drank less than three drinks a day, it makes sense to try to stay within these limits if you are a man. For women, research has shown that one alcoholic drink a day lowers the risk of coronary heart disease. For postmenopausal women, the protective effect of moderate drinking is considered to be due, in part, to an increase in estrogen levels induced by the alcohol.

If you are planning to drive, the only safe drink is a nonalcoholic one. You should also try not to drink during pregnancy because even occasional drinking has been associated with birth defects.

6 rules for safe drinking

1 Men: drink no more than 3 units a day

2 Women: drink no more than 1 unit a day

3 Don't consume a whole week's allowance in one go

4 Have at least two alcohol-free days a week

5 Only drink good quality wine

6 At a party, alternate alcoholic drinks with water

A HALF-PINT OF LAGER IS ONE UNIT

ONE GLASS OF WINE IS ONE UNIT

ONE SHOT GLASS (1FL OZ/25ML) OF SPIRITS IS ONE UNIT

ONE GLASS OF CHAMPAGNE IS ONE UNIT

Women's
Health

From anemia and mood swings to PMT and menstrual irregularities, many health problems that affect women can be greatly helped by adjusting the diet. The biggest breakthrough in women's health is the discovery of phytochemicals—substances found in particularly female-friendly foods such as soy, broccoli, and citrus fruits, which can help prevent and even reverse many conditions. These substances include phytoestrogens, which are helping women worldwide to regulate their hormones naturally.

Herbs for Women

Chaste berry (or agnus castus), wild yam, black cohosh, motherwort, raspberry, licorice, lady's mantle, and alfalfa are the eight most important herbs used to manage women's health problems including PMS, menstrual irregularities, infertility, and menopause. Some can be used in food *(see also page 62)*.

Vital compounds called phytoestrogens (or isoflavones), found naturally in foods, help to balance female hormones throughout the three main stages of women's lives.

Phytoestrogens all have an estrogenic activity that is similar to the body's own estrogen, but much less potent (only about 1/1,000th as strong). It is believed that phytoestrogens can protect the body from excess estrogen, which otherwise leads to an increased risk of uterine and breast cancer. They are thought to work by supplanting the stronger estrogen produced by the ovaries, causing it to be broken down by the liver and flushed out of the body.

From the late thirties to the end of menopause, estrogen production slowly declines. The phytoestrogens have a role to play at this time, because they act as a natural estrogen supplement, easing menopausal symptoms.

Population studies have shown that hormone-dependent diseases, including breast cancer, prostate cancer, and osteoporosis, are all much lower in those populations whose diets are highest in phytoestrogens. Asian women, for example, who traditionally eat a diet that is high in soy, which is a powerful phytoestrogen, report so few menopausal symptoms that until relatively recently, linguistic experts could not find a word in their vocabulary that equated to the hot flushes which are all too familiar to women who eat high-fat, low-fiber diets. These magical substances, which can make all the difference between good health and debilitating health problems, are readily available in a wide range of everyday

foods—soybeans, chickpeas, lentils, citrus fruits, cruciferous vegetables such as broccoli, Brussels sprouts, cabbage, and cauliflower, and licorice, onions, garlic, and chives. We have featured as many as possible in our recipes and if you do nothing else for your health, try to eat broccoli and cabbage at least once a week.

FEMALE-FRIENDLY FOODS

One of the most important phytoestrogens, and the one which has been studied the most, is called genistein. Found only in soy, it has remarkable anticancer properties. It not only inhibits tumor growth but, according to Japanese scientists, it also blocks the signal that triggers cells in the body to start multiplying so wildly out of control in the first place.

Genistein has been shown to destroy leukemia cells in mice. It acts in a similar way to tamoxifen, the drug that is given to breast-cancer patients, but, as with all the natural

soybeans, a staple ingredient in Asian cuisines, have helped to keep breast cancer and other diseases that plague Western women at bay.

phytochemicals, there are no side effects. To benefit from this potent protection, eat at least one soy product every day.

Women need more iron than men. Legumes, peas, and leafy greens will all boost your iron intake. Liver is a good source, but it is high in cholesterol, making chicken a better bet. If you are worried you may be anemic, get yourself tested because it is not easy to absorb all the iron you need from food. If you are iron-deficient, remember that vitamin C boosts iron uptake, so supplement your diet with 1g a day.

NO MORE DIETING

One national survey in the United States found that 40 percent of women were trying to lose weight—almost twice the number of men. Constant and yo-yo dieting leave women at risk of becoming malnourished. Also, if you follow a strict calorie-controlled diet, the chances are depressingly high that the weight will all pile back on when you stop.

It is better to throw out the scales and start getting back the shape you want by regulating your eating habits. Eat three meals a day and, if you feel hungry in between, snack on fresh fruit, nuts, seeds, and vegetables.

Push your shopping cart past the tempting but highly processed foods stacked on the supermarket shelves and make a beeline instead for the peripheral areas that display the fruits and vegetables. Fruits and vegetables are not the poor relations here. These are the foods that will work with you and help you lose weight. If you introduce regular, moderate exercise three times a week into your schedule, with a rest day between your exertions, your weight will quickly stabilize. And if you stick to your new, healthier eating habits, the excess pounds will stay off.

I don't know how much I weigh and I don't really care. I monitor whether I am eating too little or too much by how my clothes fit. Dump the scales, adopt the holistic healthy eating guidelines at the start of this book, and you and your family will never look back.

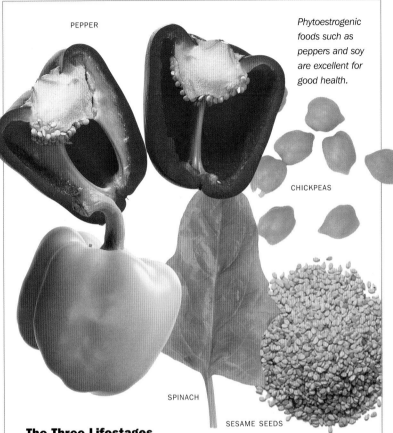

PEPPER

CHICKPEAS

SPINACH

SESAME SEEDS

Phytoestrogenic foods such as peppers and soy are excellent for good health.

The Three Lifestages

Any hormone-related disturbances you may suffer will vary depending on your age. Premenopausal women may complain of PMS, irregular menstruation, scanty or heavy periods, bloating, depression, irritability, breast tenderness, food cravings, pelvic cramps, and an altered libido from up to 14 days before their period starts.

The hormonal balance changes in what is called perimenopause. The age this starts depends on many factors, including genetic makeup, lifestyle, diet, the number of children you have had, and the amount of stress in your life. Generally, the first signs appear sometime between the mid-thirties and late forties. Periods may become either more or less frequent and you may have chronic fatigue, weight gain, water retention, mood swings, erratic blood sugar levels, and insomnia. During menopause, estrogen levels

fall by up to 60 percent and the secretion of progesterone stops. Tell-tale symptoms can include hot sweats, vaginal dryness, water retention, weight gain, insomnia, mood swings, dry and thin skin, brittle bones, fatigue, headaches, disturbed sleep patterns, and a loss of sex drive.

All of the above symptoms, in the three stages of womanhood, can be alleviated by eating a healthy diet that contains phyto-estrogenic foods.

Men's Health

Men often only consider their health when something goes wrong—they frequently look after their cars better than their own bodies. This is most unfortunate because men's health has never been more at risk: rates of prostate cancer are rising, sperm counts have fallen dramatically, and heart disease, which is often closely linked to poor lifestyle and dietary choices, is still the biggest killer of men worldwide.

Space travel has taught us valuable lessons about diet: overrefined food gave astronauts heart rhythm irregularities.

So much folklore relating to food is true. Oysters, for example, really are aphrodisiac. Researchers have found that a man's sex drive can drop dramatically even if he is only marginally deficient in zinc, since this mineral is crucial to the production of the male sex hormone testosterone. And what are oysters a rich source of? Zinc. As well as being crucial for testosterone, zinc is also needed by the prostate gland, which makes seminal fluid for semen. It needs ten times more zinc than any other organ.

A healthy prostate weighs about 1oz (25g) and is the size of a small walnut. It can, though, enlarge painfully to the size of a plum. Although rare among men who eat foods rich in zinc and omega-3 fatty acids, prostate problems currently affect 10 percent of all 40-year-olds and 80 percent of all 80-year-olds. Prostate cancer is now the second most common cancer in British men, with only lung cancer causing more deaths. So, if longevity is your goal, start taking steps to protect against prostate conditions from your late thirties onward. The good news is that there is a lot you can do. In one study of 200 men suffering from an inflamed prostate gland (a condition known as prostatitis), daily zinc supplements relieved the symptoms in 70 percent of sufferers. In that 70 percent, the prostate returned to normal or near-normal size within a few months.

Selenium has also been shown to help this condition. A study, published in the British journal *BJU International*, reported that men who took 200mcg of selenium each day were 63 percent less likely to get prostate cancer than those who did not. What is worrying is that the selenium intake of most men falls way below this level. The average intake of many men is often just 30–40mcg per day, less than a quarter of the recommended amount.

PEAK PERFORMANCE

Even impotence can be treated naturally. The best aphrodisiac, of course, is simply good health. But when 60 sufferers who had exhausted conventional treatments started taking 60mg a day of the potent Chinese herb *Ginkgo biloba*, half regained full potency within six months. The herb works by restoring circulation to all parts of the body. Both nettle and pumpkin are also said to help maintain healthy levels of male sex hormones.

MINERALS FOR HEART HEALTH

Heart disease is still the single biggest killer of men around the world, with some form of cardiovascular disease now affecting one in five American men and one in four British men. Minerals and vitamins play a crucial role in the healthy functioning of the heart for both sexes. The flow of calcium, sodium, and potassium in and out of the body's cells creates electrical currents and these "charges" then travel along the nerves to "fire" the heartbeat. Vitamin E is involved in the transportation of calcium between

Herbs for Men

Saw palmetto, *the* herb for prostate health, helps to regulate hormonal changes that can lead to an enlarged prostate gland. It reduces conversion of the hormone testosterone to dihydrotesterone, a compound that stimulates production of prostate cancer cells. Take 3 x 500mg capsules of powdered herb per day to avoid benign prostate hypertrophy (BPH), or to help relieve symptoms if you already have the condition.

cells. A deficiency in this important antioxidant has been shown to lower the heart's resistance to calcium, resulting in irregular beats. Vitamin E-rich foods include eggs, leafy greens, cold-pressed vegetable oils, almonds, hazelnuts, pecans, sunflower seeds, and sweet potatoes.

Magnesium is also important in the maintenance of a healthy heart because it helps to control the calcium and magnesium that pass through it. In fact, this mineral is so effective at keeping the heart pumping that heart-attack patients have magnesium injected into their bloodstream when they arrive in the emergency room to reduce the chances of deadly arrhythmias (irregular heartbeats).

Thanks to space travel and NASA's researchers, we now know the importance of potassium in heart health. Like magnesium, potassium affects the all-important heart rhythm. When two of the Apollo 15 astronauts, David Scott and James Irwin, both developed irregular heartbeats during a lunar

OYSTERS

mission, scientists worked out that the cause was a serious deficiency in potassium. Their food, which had been superrefined to keep it light, did not provide any of this vital mineral. Learning from this valuable lesson, when Apollo 16 was launched, the crew, who had been eating a potassium-loaded preflight diet, went into orbit with potassium-enriched foods and snacks.

In many refined foods, much of the potassium has been replaced by sodium, so you should compensate by eating plenty of potassium-rich fruit and vegetables.

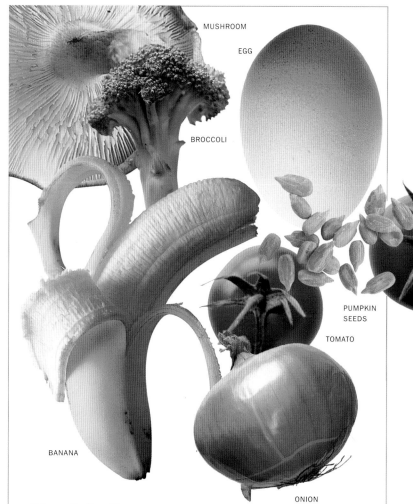

MUSHROOM

EGG

BROCCOLI

PUMPKIN SEEDS

TOMATO

BANANA

ONION

Minerals for Men

Zinc: Best food sources of zinc, which is vital for cell membranes and testosterone production, include oysters, pumpkin and sunflower seeds, organic meat, mushrooms, eggs, wholegrain products, and brewer's yeast.

Selenium: Needed to make proteins, it is also a constituent of sperm, so deficiency may be linked to infertility. Other signs of selenium deficiency include a depressed immune system, hair loss, and chest pains. Food sources include wheat germ, bran, tuna, onions, tomatoes, broccoli, kidney, and whole-wheat bread.

Magnesium: Essential for every biochemical process, including making protein and nucleic acids. Deficiency is common, especially in heavy drinkers and those who overexercise. Symptoms include weakness, fatigue, vertigo, muscle cramps, nervousness, and hyperactivity in children. To prevent a magnesium deficiency eat brown rice, soybeans, nuts, brewer's yeast, whole-wheat flour, and legumes.

Potassium: Critical for energy production and a healthy heartbeat. Sweating induced by heavy exercise may cause a loss of potassium. Symptoms of deficiency include vomiting, abdominal distension, muscular weakness, loss of appetite, low blood pressure, and intense thirst. Eat fresh fruits, particularly bananas, and plenty of vegetables such as broccoli.

Section**Two**

THE RECIPES

"In India, those who prepare the family food are dedicated to their art and valued for their skill. Here, food and God (or Brahman) are one and the same. Preparing food thoughtlessly or ineptly is regarded as sacrilege. Those who prepare food have the Well-being of the whole household in their hands, for the sages say if we prepare food while harboring angry or destructive thoughts, the food turns to poison."

Carrie Angus, *Food For The Wise*

KEY TO RECIPES AND BODY FUNCTIONS

Each recipe on the following pages has a series
of numbers to show which body systems the
ingredients in the dish will benefit or which
ailments they will help to counteract. For example,
the numbers 1, 2, and 6 by a recipe denote that
the dish will boost the immune system, digestion,
and energy levels. The numbers 8 and 9 by a
recipe indicate that the ingredients will help to
prevent cancer or stress. The full list is as follows:

❶	Immune system	❻	Energy
❷	Digestion	❼	Depression
❸	Skin and allergies	❽	Cancer
❹	Heart and blood	❾	Stress
❺	Teeth and bones	❿	Hormones

SOUPS

Roasted Squash Soup with Fenugreek and Apple

When the high betacarotene content of this soup is converted to vitamin A in the liver, it can help to protect against heart disease and cancer. Fenugreek, which can help fight asthma, will also help lower cholesterol and aid digestion.

SERVES 6

2 tbsp fenugreek powder

4 acorn squash, quartered and deseeded

3 tbsp olive oil

1 large onion, diced

1in (2.5cm) fresh root ginger, grated

3 garlic cloves, crushed

2 cooking apples, peeled and diced

4 cups (1 liter) chicken stock

freshly ground black pepper

juice of 1 lemon

1 Sprinkle half the fenugreek powder over the squash quarters and roast them in a very hot oven for 10 minutes.

2 Heat the olive oil in a large, heavy-based pan and add the rest of the fenugreek with the onion, ginger, and garlic, cooking until slightly golden.

3 Remove the squash from the oven and scoop the flesh out of the skins. Add the flesh to the pan along with the diced apple, chicken stock, and black pepper.

4 bring to a boil, then lower the heat and simmer for 40 minutes.

5 When cooked, blend, and then return to the heat to warm through. Just before serving, stir in the lemon juice.

6 Check the seasoning and dilute with fresh, organic apple juice if you prefer a less bulky texture. Serve hot with warm crusty bread.

FAT: 11G (17%) • PROTEIN: 6G (12%) • CARBOHYDRATE: 47G (16%) • FIBER: 11G (45%)
VITAMIN A: 240% • VITAMIN C: 35% • CALCIUM: 10% • CHOLESTEROL: 0

Nettle and Sorrel Soup

Nettles were once so widely used in healing that whole fields were turned over to growing them outside medieval towns and villages. Rich in iron, they help build blood and can boost both circulation and energy levels. Sorrel is an excellent antioxidant. A gentle liver tonic, this soup will also aid digestion, but avoid it if you suffer from rheumatism, kidney stones, or gout.

SERVES 6   ❷❹❻❾

8 cups (400g) fresh nettles

5 cups (250g) fresh sorrel

4 tbsp butter (or soy substitute)

3 large shallots, diced

4 tbsp organic white flour

6 cups (1.5 liters) stock (chicken or vegetable)

pinch of freshly grated nutmeg

freshly ground black pepper

juice of 1 large lemon

⅞ cup (200ml) cream (or soy substitute)

1 Bring a large, heavy-based pan of water to the boil and blanch the nettles and the sorrel for 3–4 minutes. Drain, squeeze out all the liquid, and blend to a smooth paste in a food processor.

2 In another large, heavy-based pan, heat the butter, add the shallots, and cook until soft. Add the flour and cook for 3 minutes, taking care not to let the mixture discolor.

3 Stir in the nettle and sorrel paste, the stock, nutmeg, and seasoning, and cook for 8 minutes. Just before serving, add the lemon juice.

4 Pour into warmed bowls and decorate with a swirl of cream (or cream substitute). Serve with warm Pumpkin Bread (*see page 122*).

FAT: 16G (24%) • PROTEIN: 5G (10%) • CARBOHYDRATE: 14G (5%)
FIBER: 3G (14%) • FOLATE: 100% • VITAMIN C: 70% • IRON: 20%
CHOLESTEROL: 15%

Aigo-Boulido (Creamy Garlic) Soup

The ancient Egyptians fed garlic to the workers who built the pyramids, knowing only that it was a kind of miracle cure-all. In fact, it is a powerful antibiotic and good for the heart— two or three cloves a day can reduce your risk of a heart attack. By boosting immunity, garlic can protect against colds. It is also said to have potent anticancer properties.

SERVES 6   ❶❷❸❹❼❾

12 garlic cloves, crushed

2 tbsp olive oil

4 cups (1 liter) chicken (or vegetable) stock

1 bay leaf

4 tbsp fresh sage leaves, finely chopped

3 egg yolks

freshly ground black pepper

10 slices French baguette

1 Blend the garlic and the olive oil to form a smooth paste.

2 Bring the stock to the boil in a large, heavy-based pan and add the garlic paste, bay leaf, and sage. bring to a boil, reduce the heat, and simmer for 15 minutes.

3 In a small bowl, whisk the egg yolks together with a little of the soup, then add the mixture to the pan, stirring constantly. Season to taste.

4 Broil the slices of French baguette and serve the soup with these slices floating on the top. (To make a more substantial dish, you can add boiled potatoes.)

FAT: 9G (14%) • PROTEIN: 5G (10%) • CARBOHYDRATE: 14G (5%) • FIBER: 5G (19%)
VITAMIN A: 15% • CALCIUM: 15% • IRON: 20% • CHOLESTEROL: 36%

Monkfish, Leek, and Saffron Soup

Fish is an excellent source of heart-protecting potassium and cancer-fighting selenium. It also contains the essential fatty acids, omega-6 and omega-3, that your body cannot make but must get from your diet. The healthiest ratio of these fats is 5:1 in favor of omega-6: this dish provides the perfect proportions in that ratio.

SERVES 6   ❶❸❹❽❾

1 medium-sized orange	**1lb 8oz (700g) monkfish tails, cut into 2cm (½in) pieces**
10 strands of saffron	
2 tbsp olive oil	**4 cups (1 liter) fish stock**
1 large onion, finely diced	**freshly ground black pepper**
6 leeks, sliced	
3 garlic cloves, crushed	**6 sprigs of fresh chervil, to garnish**
1¼ cups (300ml) white wine	

1 Remove a thin layer of orange rind with a vegetable peeler. Add the saffron to a little boiling water and let it infuse.
2 Heat the olive oil in a heavy-based pan and, when hot, add the onion, leeks, and garlic. Cook, stirring, until the vegetables are soft but not discolored.
3 Add three-quarters of the fish, and the white wine, orange peel, fish stock, and saffron strands, together with their water. Leave to simmer gently for 30 minutes.
4 When cooked, skim the orange peel off the surface, then blend the soup until smooth and creamy.
5 Return to the pan and add the reserved monkfish. Simmer gently for six minutes. Season and sprinkle with chervil leaves. Eat with crusty whole-wheat bread.

> FAT: 49ɢ (75%) • PROTEIN: 22ɢ (44%) • CARBOHYDRATE: 10ɢ (3%)
> FIBER: 1ɢ (5%) • VITAMIN C: 15% • OMEGA-6 FATTY ACIDS: 5.5ɢ
> POTASSIUM: 149% • SELENIUM: 67% • CHOLESTEROL: 10%

Shiitake Soup

Brown, beefy shiitake mushrooms have been eaten for more than 2,000 years in Japan. They stimulate the immune system to produce more interferon—a substance that helps the body to fend off both viral attacks and cancer. Shiitake mushrooms, which do not lose their nutritional value when cooked, help lower blood cholesterol and are also a good source of vitamin D, which in turn boosts the absorption of bone-building calcium.

SERVES 6   ❶❹❺❾

1 cup (250g) smoked tofu, diced	*For the stock:*
1½ cups (125g) shiitake mushrooms, sliced	**2 dried chilies, chopped**
	3 tbsp tamarind pulp
4 tbsp fresh cilantro, chopped	**kaffir lime leaves**
	1 onion, chopped
1 bunch fresh watercress, chopped	**1 lemon grass stalk**
1 medium-sized red chili, sliced, to garnish	**1in (2.5cm) fresh root ginger, grated**
	4 cups (1 liter) water

1 Boil all the stock ingredients together for 10 minutes. Drain through a fine sieve. Reserve the liquid and discard the contents of the sieve.
2 Stir-fry the tofu in a wok for a few minutes, then add the stock, shiitake mushrooms, and cilantro. Boil for 5 minutes.
3 Add the watercress and cook for another 2 minutes. Serve very hot with slices of fresh red chili on top.

For variety, you can also make this soup with oyster mushrooms instead of shiitake.

> FAT: 1.5ɢ (3%) • PROTEIN: 4ɢ (8%) • CARBOHYDRATE: 11ɢ (4%) • FIBER: 1ɢ (6%)
> VITAMIN C: 25% • VITAMIN D: 27.6% • CHOLESTEROL: 0

Cannellini Bean Soup

Beans are a rich source of soluble fiber, which helps to remove fat from the wall of the colon, flush out toxins from the body, lower cholesterol, and stabilize blood-sugar levels. It can help to prevent cancer of the colon, constipation, hemorrhoids, and obesity. Cabbage contains high levels of vitamin C, which is a powerful antioxidant that can help fight cancer too.

SERVES 6

2 cups (400g) dried cannellini beans

2 tbsp chopped fresh sage

1 red onion

2 garlic cloves, finely chopped

2 tbsp olive oil

3½oz (100g) pancetta, diced

2 tbsp cumin seeds

1 medium-sized white cabbage, sliced into strips

4 cups (1 liter) chicken (or vegetable) stock

1 bay leaf

4 tbsp fresh flat-leaf parsley, chopped

freshly ground black pepper

1 Soak the beans for 24 hours and then place in a large pan full of water. Add the sage and half the red onion, roughly cut. bring to a boil and simmer for 1–1½ hours until tender. Dice the rest of the onion.

2 In a large, heavy-based pan, fry the diced onion and the garlic in the olive oil until tender. They should be a golden color.

3 Add the pancetta, cumin seeds, and white cabbage to the pan and cook, stirring, for 3–4 minutes.

4 Add the cooked beans, stock, bay leaf, and parsley. Season and cook for another 20 minutes. Serve with garlic and rosemary French bread. (To make: crush 4 cloves of garlic and 4 sprigs fresh rosemary in 3 tbsp olive oil. Slice a French baguette lengthwise. Spread the garlic paste on the cut side and broil. Cut into portions.)

FAT: 57G (46%) • PROTEIN: 12G (24%) • CARBOHYDRATE: 28G (9%) • FIBER: 11G (42%)
VITAMIN C: 140% CALCIUM: 30% • IRON: 45% • CHOLESTEROL: 5%

Broiled Figs with Parma Ham and Watercress

High-fiber figs have been shown to help shrink cancer tumors. Their juice also helps digestion, acting as a natural laxative. Both figs and watercress are good sources of beta-carotene, which is converted into vitamin A in the body. This vitamin, which is a powerful antioxidant, can protect against cancers, skin disorders (including acne), and eye problems.

SERVES 6

6 fresh figs

2 tsp olive oil

2 bunches fresh watercress, chopped

10 fresh mint leaves, chopped

6 slices Parma ham, cut into strips

2oz (60g) fresh Parmesan cheese

For the dressing:

2 tsp balsamic vinegar

4 tsp olive oil

1 tsp pesto sauce

freshly ground black pepper

1 Cut the figs in half lengthwise, brush them with olive oil and cook, skin-side up, on a griddle pan for 2 minutes. Keep warm.

2 To make the dressing, mix the balsamic vinegar with the olive oil and pesto sauce. Season to taste.

3 Arrange the watercress and mint leaves on a large, flat serving dish. Place the broiled figs on the bed of leaves and arrange slices of Parma ham on the top. Drizzle the dressing over the whole dish.

4 Using a vegetable peeler, shave slices of Parmesan cheese over the ham and figs and serve.

Vegetarians can serve this dish without the meat. For variety, meat-eaters can substitute chorizo (Spanish sausage) or smoked chicken.

FAT: 14G (14%) • PROTEIN: 10G (20%) • CARBOHYDRATE: 12G (4%) • FIBER: 3G (10%)
VITAMIN A: 25% • VITAMIN C: 15% • CALCIUM: 20% • CHOLESTEROL: 10%

APPETIZERS

Marinated Raw Vegetables with Olive Oil and Herbs

Everyone knows that raw vegetables provide plenty of fiber, but did you know you can get iron and copper from mushrooms? Or that fennel provides plenty of potassium, which is needed to regulate blood pressure? This dish also provides vitamin B_6, which is crucial for healthy blood and for making antibodies to fight disease. Loaded with vitamin A, it is a simple but potent anticancer recipe.

SERVES 6

1 large fennel bulb, cut into 2in (5cm) strips	**freshly ground black pepper**
1 red pepper, cut into 2in (5cm) strips	*For the marinade:*
1 green pepper, cut into 2in (5cm) strips	**5 garlic cloves, chopped**
5 stalks celery, cut into 2in (5cm) strips	**½ cup (125ml) olive oil**
2 carrots, cut into 2in (5cm) strips	**2 drops Tabasco sauce**
3 cups (250g) button mushrooms	**6 tbsp white wine vinegar**
2 shallots, sliced into rings	**2 tbsp chopped fresh chives**
3 tbsp small capers	**2 tbsp chopped fresh chervil**
4 tbsp black olives, pitted	**2 tbsp chopped fresh cilantro**

1 Mix all the vegetables, the shallots, capers, and olives, together in a large, flat glass dish.
2 To make the marinade, combine all the ingredients, reserving a quarter of the chopped herbs for a garnish. Pour over the vegetable mix, making sure all the vegetable strips are completely covered. Refrigerate for at least 12 hours.
3 Just before serving, sprinkle the reserved fresh herbs over the vegetables and season. Serve with warmed ciabatta bread.

This dish can form the base for a range of appetizers and supper dishes. You can also mix it with whole-wheat pasta or couscous for a picnic lunch.

FAT: 22G (34%) • PROTEIN: 3G (6%) • CARBOHYDRATE: 13G (4%)
FIBER: 4G (17%) • VITAMIN A: 120% • VITAMIN B6: 13%
VITAMIN C: 80% • IRON: 10% • POTASSIUM: 64% • CHOLESTEROL: 0

Broiled Mackerel with Green Sauce

Protein-rich and high in immune-boosting and cancer-fighting vitamin C, this dish also provides omega-3, an essential fatty acid that has been shown to shrink cancer tumors and protect against lung, breast, and prostate cancers. Fatty acids, which are typically missing from most Western diets, can also boost memory and reduce the severity of migraine headaches in some sufferers.

SERVES 6

6 small mackerel, scaled and gutted	**1 tsp ground cumin**
1 large onion, roughly chopped	**juice of 2 fresh limes**
5 garlic cloves	**1in (2.5cm) piece fresh root ginger, chopped**
5 fresh green chilies	**1 tsp sugar (optional)**
6 tbsp fresh coconut flesh	**1 tsp salt**
4 tbsp fresh cilantro, chopped	

1 Slash the mackerel three times diagonally on each side. Put all the other ingredients in a food processor and blend to make a smooth paste.
2 Baste the fish with the paste and broil under a medium heat for 5–7 minutes on each side, until the green sauce coating starts to bubble and the fish flesh flakes easily. The sugar will make the sauce shiny but is optional.

You can also use red snapper, sardines, or salmon fillets.

FAT: 13G (19%) • PROTEIN: 82G (164%) • CARBOHYDRATE: 10G (3%)
FIBER: 3G (10%) • VITAMIN A: 70% • VITAMIN C: 170% • IRON: 45%
CHOLESTEROL: 70%

Shiitake Paté

Used in clinical trials to boost the immune response of HIV patients, shiitake mushrooms contain a polysaccharide called lentinan, which has been shown to slow the growth of cancerous tumors in animals. They also lower cholesterol and help to prevent heart disease. Magnesium, known as the anti-stress mineral, is provided mainly by the shiitake mushrooms.

SERVES 4–6 ① ② ③ ④ ⑤ ⑥ ⑨ ⑩

3½oz (100g) fresh or dried shiitake mushrooms

2 tsp sesame seeds

1 large potato, cut into chunks

1 tsp sesame oil

3 large shallots, diced

2 tsp low-fat yogurt

juice of 1 lemon

2 tsp soy sauce

freshly ground black pepper

1 If you are using dried mushrooms, soak them in hot water for 20 minutes. If using fresh mushrooms, clean them with a small vegetable brush. Slice or dice the mushrooms.

2 In a dry pan, quickly brown the sesame seeds. Boil the potato chunks for 15–20 minutes, or until tender. Heat the sesame oil in a wok and cook the mushrooms and shallots until slightly brown.

3 When all the ingredients are cooked, put them in a food processor with the low-fat yogurt, lemon juice, soy sauce and browned sesame seeds. Blend until puréed. Season and chill for 2 hours before serving. Serve with warm mixed grain toast.

FAT: 2.5G (4%) • PROTEIN: 5G (10%) • CARBOHYDRATE: 31G (10%)
FIBER: 4G (17%) • VITAMIN C: 20% • MAGNESIUM: 20% • CHOLESTEROL: 0

Broiled Goats' Cheese on Lambs' Lettuce

A healthy immune and nervous system both depend on manganese, which also helps regulate the sex hormones, brain function and blood-sugar levels. Bread is an excellent source. The goats' cheese provides selenium, a powerful antioxidant, which plays a crucial role in prostate health.

SERVES 6 ① ② ④ ⑤ ⑦ ⑧ ⑨

2 medium-sized cooking apples, cored and diced

1 pinch of cinnamon

12 slices of granary/mixed grain bread

7oz (200g) goats' cheese, cut into 12 rounds

14oz (400g) lambs' lettuce salad leaves

1 raw beet, grated

For the dressing:

4 tbsp vinegar

1 garlic clove, crushed

freshly ground black pepper

1 tsp wholegrain mustard

1 tsp honey

½ cup (125ml) olive oil

1 Put the apple and cinnamon in a pan with 2 tbsp water. Cook gently for 10 minutes until puréed, then let cool.

2 Cut 12 disks from the granary bread with a round cutter. Spread the apple purée over the bread disks, place the cheese on top, and arrange on a flat baking sheet.

3 To make the salad dressing, mix together the vinegar, garlic, pepper, mustard, and honey. Add the olive oil, whisking constantly.

4 Put the goats' cheese toast under the broiler and cook until the cheese is melted and golden brown.

5 Toss the salad leaves and the grated beet thoroughly with the dressing. Arrange on a flat dish and place the goats' cheese toast on top.

FAT: 30G (46%) • PROTEIN: 12G (24%) • CARBOHYDRATE: 35G (12%)
FIBER: 8G (31%) • MAGNESIUM: 14% • MANGANESE: 7.6% • SELENIUM: 1.6%
CHOLESTEROL: 10%

Marinated Sardines with Pine Nuts

Sardines are the richest natural source of omega-3 fatty acids, which can help prevent arthritis and breast cancer. Pine nuts are a good source, too. The fish also provides vitamin B_{12}, which can improve memory and is essential for fertility and for building healthy blood and tissue.

SERVES 6   ② ③ ④ ⑦ ⑩

12 fresh sardine fillets, boned and scaled	*For the sauce:*
	6 garlic cloves
freshly ground black pepper	4 tbsp pine nuts
½ cup (125ml) olive oil	1 tsp chopped fresh basil
juice of 3 large lemons	4 tbsp olive oil
3 tbsp chopped fresh basil	juice of 1 lemon
	1 pinch cayenne pepper

1 Lay the sardine fillets skin-side up in a dish and season. Mix together the olive oil, lemon juice, and chopped basil (reserving a little for the garnish). Pour over the top of the fish and chill for at least 3 hours. The acid in the lemon juice "cooks" the fish.

2 Meanwhile, make the sauce. Place all the ingredients in a food processor, season, and blend until smooth. Check the seasoning and chill.

3 When the fillets are ready the flesh will have changed from brown to white. Serve them on slices of thick toasted brown bread, garnished with chopped basil and with the sauce on the side in a ramekin.

> FAT: 24G (38%) • PROTEIN: 13G (26%) • CARBOHYDRATE: 4G (1%)
> FIBER: 1G (8%) • VITAMIN B_3: 37% • VITAMIN B_{12}: 261%
> VITAMIN C 15% • CHOLESTEROL: 11%

Tartare of Salmon with Lime Juice

The Japanese, who regularly eat raw fish, have some of the lowest rates of heart disease in the world. The potassium in the salmon will help lower blood pressure, flush out toxins, regulate heartbeat, and alleviate allergies. Stress, coffee, alcohol, and sugar all deplete the body's potassium levels, so it is important to eat potassium-rich foods regularly.

SERVES 6   ① ③ ④ ⑨

14oz (400g) salmon fillet	juice of 3 limes
4 tomatoes	1 tsp fresh basil, chopped
freshly ground black pepper	1 tsp fresh parsley, chopped
1 tsp green peppercorns	½ cup (125ml) olive oil
2 large shallots, diced	4 tbsp low-fat yogurt

1 Skin and bone the salmon fillet or ask your fishmonger to do it for you. Dice the salmon finely and reserve in the refrigerator. Steep the tomatoes in boiling water for 1 minute. Remove, skin, and dice them.

2 In a large bowl, combine the diced salmon, pepper, green peppercorns, and shallots. Add the lime juice, half the chopped basil, the parsley, the low-fat yogurt and half of the olive oil. Leave to stand in the refrigerator for an hour.

3 Mix the diced tomatoes with the rest of the basil and olive oil to create the sauce. Place the salmon mixture in the middle of a plate with the tomatoes around it. Sprinkle with freshly ground black pepper.

For a Thai-style taste, substitute coconut milk for the low-fat yogurt.

> FAT: 34G (52%) • PROTEIN: 22G (44%) • CARBOHYDRATE: 15G (5%)
> FIBER: 3G (12%) • VITAMIN C: 50% • IRON: 15% • POTASSIUM: 50%
> CHOLESTEROL: 12%

Asian-Style Oysters with Spinach

Oysters are the richest food source of zinc, which protects not only the prostate, but all the reproductive organs. It also helps to prevent acne, boosts the immune system, and accelerates wound-healing. Zinc works best in tandem with the anticancer, antioxidant vitamin A, which is supplied in abundance by this recipe. The presence of zinc increases the absorption of vitamin A. The spinach acts as a general blood tonic and will aid digestion.

SERVES 6

12 large oysters

12 large spinach leaves

2 carrots, cut into long strips

3 leeks, cut into long strips

2 tbsp soy cream

1 pinch of curry powder

freshly ground black pepper

2 tbsp fresh chervil

2 cups (200g) sea salt to rest the oysters on for cooking: do not eat

1 Clean the oysters. Open them and pass the juice through a fine sieve. Remove the hard stalks of the spinach, wash the leaves and blanch (cook briefly) for a few minutes in boiling water. When softened, place the wilted leaves on a clean tea towel to drain.

2 Detach the oysters from their shells and wrap them in the middle of a spinach leaf. Return them to their original shells, pouring a little of their juice back over them.

3 Cook the carrots and leeks for about 5 minutes in boiling water, or until tender. Put the sea salt in an ovenproof dish and arrange the oysters on top. Place them in a warm oven (275°F/140°C/Gas 1) and cook for 5 minutes.

4 When cooked, pour the juice off each oyster into a pan. Add the soy cream, curry powder, and black pepper. Bring to a boil and simmer for 1 minute to reduce the sauce.

5 To serve, place two oysters on each plate and pour a little of the sauce over each oyster. Pile the cooked vegetables and the chervil high on top. Serve with nutty rye bread.

FAT: 5G (7%) • PROTEIN: 13G (26%) • CARBOHYDRATE: 12G (4%) • FIBER: 1G (6%)
VITAMIN A: 120% • IRON: 70% • ZINC: 100% • CHOLESTEROL: 30%

SALADS

Chickpea, Lime, and Cilantro Salad

Lime, coriander, and to some extent, chickpeas are good sources of vitamin C, which is crucial for the growth and repair of body tissues and which also helps the body to absorb iron. It accelerates healing after surgery, wards off the common cold, and helps lower blood cholesterol. This recipe is particularly helpful if you smoke because each cigarette destroys 25mg of vitamin C. The chickpeas are also an excellent source of both fiber and potassium.

SERVES 6

5 cups (800g) dried chickpeas

1 large red onion, thinly sliced

1 red pepper, diced

1 green pepper, diced

2 tbsp fresh cilantro, chopped

For the dressing:

3 garlic cloves, crushed

½ cup (125ml) olive oil

juice of 4 limes

1 Soak the chickpeas for 12 hours and cook them in unsalted water until tender (this may take up to 4 hours, though 2 is more usual). Skim the scum from the top from time to time. Alternatively, use precooked chickpeas.
2 Combine the cooked chickpeas with the sliced onion, the diced peppers, and the chopped cilantro.
3 To make the dressing, mix together all the ingredients, then pour it over the chickpeas. Toss gently. Let the salad rest for at least 2 hours before serving. Serve with Irish wheaten bread if available, or whole-wheat bread.

FAT: 24G (34%) • PROTEIN: 27G (52%) • CARBOHYDRATE: 87G (29%) • FIBER: 100%
VITAMIN C: 150% • IRON: 50% • POTASSIUM: 160% • CHOLESTEROL: 0

Roasted Nori (Seaweed) Salad

Magnesium helps the body to burn fat and produce energy. It is frequently lacking in postmenopausal women and has also been identified as a contributory factor in premenstrual syndrome. This Japanese seaweed salad can help to restore normal levels. A fifth of elderly people who take diuretics have a sodium deficiency, which the soy sauce can help to correct.

SERVES 6

6 cups cooked white rice

1½ cups (125g) Nori, roasted (see below) and flaked

2 tsp sesame oil

1 small zucchini, grated

½ red pepper, diced

½ green pepper, diced

3 tbsp sesame seeds, toasted

2 large onions, finely diced

1in (2.5cm) piece fresh root ginger, grated

For the dressing:

6 garlic cloves, crushed

2 tbsp rice vinegar

3 tbsp soy sauce

1 tsp honey

1 To make the dressing, whisk the crushed garlic, vinegar, soy sauce, and honey in a small bowl.

2 Lay the Nori sheets flat on a baking sheet and roast in an oven at 350F°/180°C/Gas 4 for 3 minutes until crisp.

3 In a large bowl, mix the Nori and rice with all the other ingredients. Just before serving, add the dressing to the salad and serve very cold with a small side dish of Japanese rice crackers.

FAT: 5G (8%) • PROTEIN: 6G (12%) • CARBOHYDRATE: 41G (14%) • FIBER: 3G (12%)
VITAMIN C: 80% • MAGNESIUM: 33% • SODIUM: 35% • CHOLESTEROL: 0

Dandelion and Pancetta Salad

This is probably the most potent anticancer salad you will ever eat, and the main ingredient—dandelion leaves—could be growing for free in your garden. Packed with nutrients, this simple dish can help lower cholesterol and boost energy levels. It also improves the condition of your skin and helps your immune system to build potent antibodies.

SERVES 6

1 small French baguette

2 tbsp olive oil

7oz (200g) pancetta (Italian bacon), cut into strips

2 tbsp balsamic vinegar

10 cups (500g) fresh dandelion leaves, cleaned

6 tbsp fresh flat-leaf parsley, chopped, to garnish

For the dressing:

½ cup (125ml) olive oil

4 tbsp balsamic vinegar

1 tsp wholegrain mustard

1 Combine all the ingredients to make the salad dressing.

2 Cut the baguette into bite-sized cubes and sauté in olive oil until golden brown to make croûtons. Remove from the pan and leave to drain on paper towels.

3 In a griddle pan, cook the pancetta over a low heat. When golden brown, splash a few drops of balsamic vinegar into the pan to caramelize and sweet-coat the meat (deglaze). Add 3½oz (100g) croûtons, stir briefly, and remove from the heat.

4 Put the dandelion leaves in a large bowl, with the dressing. Add the pancetta and the croûtons. Serve with chopped parsley sprinkled over each portion.

FAT: 32G (49%) • PROTEIN: 13G (26%) • CARBOHYDRATE: 14G (5%)
FIBER: 2G (8%) • VITAMIN A: 160% • VITAMIN B₁₂: 34% • VITAMIN C: 60%
CHOLESTEROL: 20%

Classic Caesar Salad

The retinol (a form of vitamin A) in this dish comes from the Parmesan cheese and can enhance immunity and improve skin quality. As well as building skeletal strength, the calcium, albeit from the high-fat Parmesan, can still help lower cholesterol, provide energy, and help to relieve depression.

SERVES 6

2 bunches Romaine lettuce	*For the dressing:*
3 slices organic white bread	1 egg, beaten
4 tbsp olive oil	3 garlic cloves, crushed
12 black olives	1 tsp soy sauce
12 anchovy fillets	4 tbsp olive oil
4 tbsp fresh Parmesan cheese	juice of 1 lemon
	freshly ground black pepper

1 Wash and drain the Romaine lettuces. Cut into generous-sized pieces and arrange in a large salad bowl. Cut the sliced bread into small cubes. Heat the olive oil in a pan and sauté the cubes gently to make croûtons.

2 To make the dressing, mix the egg with the crushed garlic and soy sauce. Drizzle in the olive oil, little by little, and whisk gently. Add the lemon juice and season to taste.

3 Add the croûtons, olives, anchovies, and dressing to the Romaine lettuce leaves. Toss gently to coat them all. Use a vegetable peeler to shave fresh Parmesan onto the top of the salad and serve with a crusty French baguette.

You can also add shrimp or crisp bacon bits to this salad.

FAT: 12G (19%) • PROTEIN: 9G (18%) • CARBOHYDRATE: 4G (1%)
FIBER: 3G (10%) • VITAMIN A: 15% • CALCIUM: 20% • IRON: 10%
CHOLESTEROL: 6%

Wakame and Daikon Salad

A member of the radish family, daikon, which is also called mooli, is a long, white Japanese radish with a pungent, sweet flavor. The name means giant root and it accounts for a quarter of Japan's vegetable crop. In Chinese medicine, radishes are used to cleanse the liver and promote digestion. Wakame, a long, dark-green seaweed, is an excellent vegetarian source of vitamin B_{12}.

SERVES 6

1 medium-sized daikon	1 small red chili, sliced, to garnish
3 tsp sea salt (to leech the water from the daikon; do not eat)	*For the dressing:*
4 tbsp dried wakame	3 tsp sugar
5 tsp sesame seeds	5 tsp rice vinegar
	3 tsp Japanese soy sauce

1 Peel and cut the daikon into four pieces, lengthwise, then cut each piece very thinly into delicate slices. Lay these in a colander and sprinkle the sea salt on top. Leave for 15 minutes to leech out the fluids.

2 Soak the wakame in hot water for 10 minutes. Toast the sesame seeds (without oil) until brown.

3 Rinse the daikon slices thoroughly and squeeze out the excess water. Drain the wakame and cut very thinly.

4 To make the salad dressing, mix together the sugar, vinegar, and soy sauce.

5 In a salad bowl, combine the wakame, daikon, and the dressing. Just before serving, sprinkle the toasted sesame seeds over the top and then garnish with slices of fiery red chili.

FAT: 1.5G (2%) • PROTEIN: 1G (2%) • CARBOHYDRATE: 7G (2%)
FIBER: 1G (5%) • VITAMIN C: 50% • CALCIUM: 7% • CHOLESTEROL: 0

Marinated Roasted Mixed Peppers on a Bed of Arugula

Stress depletes the body's reserves of vitamin C, so in busy periods try this salad, which is crammed with lots of healthy nutrients, especially vitamin C. This vitamin is a powerful antioxidant and an excellent detoxifier. As well as scavenging for carcinogens and other toxins, it also helps the body to absorb blood-building iron and bone-strengthening calcium.

SERVES 6

1 large red pepper

1 large green pepper

1 large orange pepper

1 large yellow pepper

1 large black (capsicum) pepper

4 tbsp olive oil

14oz (400g) fresh arugula leaves

2 tbsp fresh basil leaves, chopped, to garnish

2 tbsp fresh sage leaves, chopped, to garnish

For the marinade:

½ cup (125ml) olive oil

4 tbsp balsamic vinegar

juice of 2 lemons

5 garlic cloves, crushed

freshly ground black pepper

1 Cut all the peppers in half lengthwise. Remove the stems and deseed them. Place them cut-side down in a roasting tray and brush each one with olive oil. Roast under a broiler or in a very hot oven until the skins blacken. Leave to cool, peel, then cut into long, thin strips.

2 Combine all the ingredients for the marinade. Check the seasoning.

3 Add the peppers to the bowl of arugula and drizzle over the marinade. Chill for at least 3 hours in the refrigerator before garnishing with basil and sage and serving with warm foccacia bread.

FAT: 1G (5%) • PROTEIN: 3G (6%) • CARBOHYDRATE: 20G (7%) • FIBER: 4G (16%)
VITAMIN A: 190% • VITAMIN C: 390% • CHOLESTEROL: 0

FISH

Cassoulet de la Mer

Present in every single cell in the body, phosphorous works with calcium to promote bone and heart health. You need to eat these minerals in a ratio of 2:1 in favor of calcium. This dish contains abundant supplies of both as well as vitamin C, which helps the body to absorb calcium and aids the excretion of toxic metals.

SERVES 6

½ cup (375ml) dried green beans

6 fresh sage leaves

freshly ground black pepper

5 strands of saffron

4 garlic cloves, crushed

1 large onion, chopped

2 fennel bulbs, chopped

4 tbsp olive oil

6 large tomatoes, skinned, deseeded, and chopped

1 star anise

1 sprig of thyme

2 bay leaves

8 cups (2 liters) fish stock

2 tbsp fresh tarragon, chopped

10½oz (300g) undyed, smoked haddock fillets

1lb 12oz (800g) sea bass fillet

12 jumbo shrimp, uncooked

1 Soak the green beans for 24 hours. Bring a pot of water to a boil and cook the beans with 3 sage leaves for 1–1½ hours, or until tender. Do not add seasoning until the end of the cooking time to avoid the skin of the beans toughening. Place the saffron in a little boiling water and let it infuse.

2 Sauté the garlic, onion, and fennel in the olive oil for 5 minutes, then add the chopped tomatoes, star anise, thyme, remaining sage, bay leaves, fish stock, and saffron, together with the water it has been infused in.

3 Transfer the sauce to an ovenproof casserole dish, add the chopped tarragon, and bring all these ingredients to a boil on the stove. Heat the oven to 325°F/160°C/Gas 3. Add the smoked haddock and sea bass to the casserole dish, place in the oven, and cook slowly for 1 hour.

4 Add the green beans and the jumbo shrimp and cook for a further 30 minutes. Season and serve with baby new potatoes.

FAT: 14G (22%) • PROTEIN: 50G (100%) • CARBOHYDRATE: 24G (8%) • FIBER: 7G (27%)
VITAMIN A: 40% • VITAMIN C: 100% • PHOSPHOROUS: 63% • CHOLESTEROL: 32%

Roasted Sea Bass with Lentils, Leeks, and a Warm Tomato Vinaigrette

No wonder they call fish brain food. Potassium, which works inside the cells to regulate heartbeat, also improves mental clarity and boosts energy levels. Lentils are high in calcium, magnesium, phosphorous, sulfur, and vitamin A and are a nutritional power food: eat a moderate portion twice a week.

SERVES 6

1¼ cups (180g) baby lentils

3 cups (700ml) chicken (or vegetable) stock

freshly ground black pepper

3 leeks, white parts only, cut into julienne strips

1 tsp olive oil

6 tbsp low-fat cream (or soy cream)

1 pinch grated nutmeg

12 x 2oz (60g) sea bass scallops (two per person)

For the vinaigrette:

½ cup (125ml) olive oil

4 tbsp balsamic vinegar

4 tomatoes, skinned, deseeded, and diced

2 tbsp fresh chives, chopped

1 Cook the lentils in the stock for about 30 minutes, or until tender. Drain, season, and put to one side.

2 Sauté the leeks gently in the olive oil until tender, but not discolored, then add the cream. Season to taste, add the nutmeg, and keep warm.

3 Season the sea bass scallops and cook them on a non-stick griddle (without oil) for 2 minutes on each side.

4 To make the tomato vinaigrette, mix the olive oil and balsamic vinegar in a small pan. Add the diced tomatoes and warm gently over a low heat. Add the chopped chives and season to taste.

5 To serve, arrange the leeks in the middle of six large plates. Place one scallop on top of each pile and cover with lentils. Balance the second scallop on top of the lentils and cover generously with the warm tomato vinaigrette.

You can replace the sea bass with salmon or monkfish fillets.

FAT: 20G (31%) • PROTEIN: 27G (54%) • CARBOHYDRATE: 18G (6%)
FIBER: 4G (17%) • VITAMIN A: 30% • VITAMIN C: 60% • CALCIUM: 8%
MAGNESIUM: 29% • PHOSPHOROUS: 42% • POTASSIUM: 81% • CHOLESTEROL: 18%

Cod Fillet with Lima Bean Mash

A low-fat saltwater fish, fresh cod is enjoying a renaissance among top chefs. It provides B vitamins, including B_1, which helps metabolize carbohydrates and aids digestion by increasing production of hydrochloric acid, needed to break down food in the stomach. This dish also contains sage which provides manganese, required by the body to metabolize vitamin C. Sage is also a good tonic for the lungs and the female reproductive system.

SERVES 6

2 cups (400g) dried lima beans

10 fresh sage leaves

1 sprig of fresh rosemary

1 small carrot

1 small onion

½ cup (125ml) olive oil

5 tsp balsamic vinegar

freshly ground black pepper

6 tomatoes

1 tsp coriander seeds

2lb 4oz (1kg) cod fillet, with skin

juice of 2 lemons

1 bunch of fresh flat-leaf parsley, to garnish

1 Soak the lima beans overnight and cook in a pan of water with the sage, rosemary, carrot, and onion for 1–1½ hours, or until tender. When cooked, drain and mash three-quarters of the beans with some of the cooking juice, discarding the herbs, carrot, and onion.

2 Add the balsamic vinegar and half of the olive oil. Season to taste. Add the rest of the beans, leaving them unmashed to provide texture.

3 Cut the tomatoes in half, lengthwise. Grease a baking sheet with olive oil, and sprinkle over the coriander seeds and seasoning. Place the tomatoes on top and cook them very slowly, with the oven on its lowest setting, for 2 hours until soft. Then quarter them, skin them, and cut the quarters in half again. Put to one side.

4 Cook the cod fillet on a nonstick griddle pan, skin-side down for 3 minutes. Season. Turn over and cook for a further 3 minutes. Season again. Splash the lemon juice into the pan to deglaze (create a caramelized sauce).

5 To serve, spoon the lima bean mash onto a large plate. Place the cod fillet on top and arrange the tomatoes around the edge. Drizzle the cooking sauce over the fish and garnish with parsley and freshly ground black pepper.

FAT: 17G (26%) • PROTEIN: 45G (90%) • CARBOHYDRATE: 18G (6%)
FIBER: 5G (19%) • VITAMIN A: 50% • VITAMIN C: 60%
MANGANESE: 24% • CHOLESTEROL: 30%

Monkfish Scallops and Oysters with Licorice Sauce

Zinc-rich oysters together with spinach brimming with carotenes, and vitamin A-rich carrots and beets, make this recipe a potent anticancer feast. As well as protecting against cancer of the prostate, zinc has recently been shown to be useful in the treatment of mental illness. Licorice has an antiviral action but can trigger water retention so avoid it if you are suffering from premenstrual syndrome (PMS).

SERVES 6

4 carrots, cut into julienne strips

6 leeks, white parts only, cut into julienne strips

6 tbsp olive oil spread

8 cups (400g) young spinach leaves

freshly ground black pepper

6 fresh oysters

6 x 6¼oz (180g) monkfish scallops

4 tbsp cooked beets, cut into fine strips

1 small bunch of fresh chervil, chopped, to garnish

For the sauce:

3 shallots, finely diced

1¾ cups (400ml) medium white wine

½ cup (125ml) reduced-fat light cream

1 pinch of licorice powder

1 Sauté the carrots and leeks in the olive oil spread over a gentle heat. Wash the spinach leaves and cook them in a pan with a tablespoon of water until wilted. Season and put to one side.

2 Open the oysters and strain the juices through a sieve. Keep the oyster flesh and juice, but discard the shells.

3 To make the sauce, cook the shallots in the white wine until three-quarters of the wine has evaporated. Add the juice from the oysters, the cream, and the licorice powder and reduce for 2 minutes.

4 Season the monkfish scallops and cook without oil on a nonstick griddle pan for 3 minutes on each side.

5 When you are ready to serve, poach the oysters in the licorice sauce for 3 minutes and warm the vegetables. Place a pile of spinach in the middle of each plate. Put a monkfish scallop on top, then an oyster, followed by some leeks, carrots, and beets. Surround the fish with the licorice sauce and sprinkle the dish with chopped chervil leaves.

FAT: 17G (27%) • PROTEIN: 33G (66%) • CARBOHYDRATE: 14G (5%)
FIBER: 4G (14%) • VITAMIN A: 250% • MANGANESE: 57% • POTASSIUM: 148%
ZINC: 64% • CHOLESTEROL: 34%

Chili Crab Cakes Singapore-Style

Copper deficiency can contribute to osteoporosis. Combat brittle bones with this dish that contains copper-rich crab meat. Crab also provides vitamin B_3 (niacin), which can help reduce cholesterol, boost energy levels, and give you healthier-looking skin.

SERVES 6

8 large potatoes, cut into chunks

3 fresh red chilies, deseeded and diced

4 dried chilies, chopped

2 tsp shrimp paste

1 lemongrass stalk, roughly chopped

10 unsalted cashew nuts

1lb 5oz (600g) crab meat

⅔ cup (100g) flour (use wheat-free if intolerant)

3 eggs, beaten

1 cup (150g) breadcrumbs

4 tbsp sesame oil, for frying

2 tbsp cilantro, chopped

For the sauce:

2 tsp sesame oil, to sauté

2 shallots, chopped

4 garlic cloves, crushed

1in (2.5cm) piece fresh root ginger, grated

2 cups (500ml) chicken stock

1 Cook the potatoes in boiling water for 15–20 minutes until soft. Mash and put to one side. In a food processor, mix together all the chilies, the shrimp paste, lemongrass, and cashew nuts to form a smooth paste.

2 Combine the crab meat with the mashed potatoes and one-third of the paste. Divide this mixture into 12 round-shaped cakes. Coat each of these first with flour, then beaten egg followed by breadcrumbs. Put to one side.

3 For the sauce, sauté the shallots, crushed garlic, and grated ginger in sesame oil for a few minutes. Add the remaining two-thirds of the chili and nut paste and cook for a few more minutes. Add the chicken stock and cook for another 2–3 minutes until the sauce has thickened.

4 Heat a shallow pool of sesame oil in a skillet and add the crab cakes. Cook over a medium heat until golden brown on both sides (about 5 minutes per side).

5 Pour the sauce onto six dinner plates and place two crab cakes in the middle of each, propped up against each other. Garnish with chopped cilantro leaves.

To serve as an appetizer, reduce to one crab cake per person. For a quick supper, replace the sauce with a squeeze of lime juice.

FAT: 23G (35%) • PROTEIN: 36G (72%) • CARBOHYDRATE: 79G (26%)
FIBER: 5G (21%) • VITAMIN B_3: 70% • VITAMIN C: 100% • COPPER: 39% • IRON: 30%
CHOLESTEROL: 59%

Carri of Tuna and Ginger

The quantity of potassium that you need, which in this dish comes from fish and vegetables, depends on how much muscle you have and your state of health, since low blood-sugar and severe stomach upsets can deplete the body's stores. Inspired by Mauritian cuisine, this recipe is ideal for people convalescing from illness and those who are very fit.

SERVES 6

½ cup (125ml) olive oil

3 large onions, sliced

6 garlic cloves, crushed

1¼in (3cm) piece fresh root ginger, grated

1 pinch of ground cumin

2lb 14½oz (1.3kg) fresh tuna, diced

7 medium tomatoes, skinned and roughly chopped

5 tsp Thai fish sauce

4 cups (1 liter) fish stock

freshly ground black pepper

1 bunch of scallions, chopped

1 To make a compote, heat half the olive oil in a large heavy-based pan. Cook the onions, garlic, and ginger until soft. Add the ground cumin and a little water and cook for 20 minutes until tender and slightly browned.
2 Seal the tuna in the remaining olive oil and transfer to the compote. Add the tomatoes, Thai fish sauce, and fish stock. Season and leave to cook very slowly for 30–40 minutes.
3 Check the seasoning again and, just before you serve, add the chopped scallions. Serve with rice.

This dish is even more delicious when reheated the following day when the flavors have had time to seep through all the ingredients. You can also make a Carri in exactly the same way with meat.

> FAT: 19G (29%) • PROTEIN: 54G (108%) • CARBOHYDRATE: 18G (6%)
> FIBER: 4G (16%) • VITAMIN A: 120% • VITAMIN C: 90% • POTASSIUM: 125%
> CHOLESTEROL: 27%

Salmon Fillet with Broiled Hazelnuts

This dish is packed with protein and the antioxidant vitamins A and C, and the hazelnuts contain manganese, which provides additional antioxidant, anticancer protection and helps to keep the brain, skeleton, circulation, and immune and nervous systems in good health. Low manganese levels are associated with atherosclerosis.

SERVES 6

1 small cauliflower head, cut into florets

1 pinch of nutmeg

2 tbsp soy cream

freshly ground black pepper

⅔ cup (125g) hazelnuts

½ cup (125ml) hazelnut or olive oil

6 x 6¼oz (180g) salmon fillets, with the skin on

5 tsp balsamic vinegar

1 tbsp chopped fresh chives, to garnish

1 Cook the cauliflower in boiling water until soft. Drain and transfer to a food processor. Blend with the nutmeg and soy cream to form a mousse. Season.
2 Place the hazelnuts in a roasting tin and bake them in a hot oven for 15 minutes until the skin slips off easily. Roughly crush them and warm them gently in a small pan with the hazelnut oil. Do not boil. Remove the nuts from the pan, reserving the oil.
3 Season the salmon fillets and cook, skin-side down on a nonstick griddle pan (no oil is necessary) for 3 minutes. Turn and cook for another 3 minutes. Keep warm.
4 To serve, place each salmon fillet on a warm plate with the hazelnuts. Drizzle some of the oil you cooked the nuts in over the fish and nuts. Splash with balsamic vinegar. To one side of the fish, add some cauliflower mousse and sprinkle chopped chives over the entire dish.

> FAT: 50G (76%) • PROTEIN: 45G (90%) • CARBOHYDRATE: 20G (7%)
> FIBER: 9G (35%) • VITAMIN A: 90% • VITAMIN C: 150% • MANGANESE: 28%
> CHOLESTEROL: 36%

Bouillabaisse

This tasty, classic fish stew is a storehouse of B vitamins and heart-protecting folic acid. It also provides more than a day's full requirement of manganese, needed for the manufacture of vitamin K, which promotes healthy blood clotting.

SERVES 6

3 large onions, chopped

3 leeks, white parts only, chopped

3 stalks of celery, chopped

6 garlic cloves, chopped

1 large fennel bulb, chopped

½ cup (125ml) olive oil

1oz (25g) orange peel

4 large tomatoes, skinned, deseeded, and chopped

1 tsp saffron powder

1 tsp fresh thyme

3 bay leaves

4 cups (1 liter) water

10½oz (300g) conger eel

10½oz (300g) monkfish

10½oz (300g) skate wings

4 tsp Pernod

3 small red mullets

10½oz (300g) Arctic sea bass

10½oz (300g) cod

1lb 2oz (500g) fresh mussels, cleaned

8 langoustines (with their shells)

1 pinch of cayenne pepper

For the croûtons:

16 slices of French baguette

3 garlic cloves

For the rouille:

6 slices French bread, cubed, soaked in milk

6 garlic cloves, crushed

1 pinch of cayenne pepper

1 pinch of saffron powder

⅞ cup (200ml) olive oil

1 To make the croûtons, broil the slices of dry French bread on both sides and rub them with fresh garlic.

2 For the rouille, blend the garlic with the cayenne pepper and saffron to form a smooth paste. Season. Squeeze and drain the French bread you have presoaked in milk and blend with the garlic paste. Add the olive oil, little by little, blending as you go. Check the seasoning.

3 To make the bouillabaisse, cook the vegetables in olive oil, until tender. Add the orange peel, tomatoes, herbs, and water. bring to a boil, then simmer for 25 minutes.

4 Put the Conger eel, monkfish, and skate in the pot with the boiling vegetables. Add the Pernod and cook for another 5 minutes. Add the rest of the fish and cook for another 7 minutes.

5 Finally, add the mussels and the langoustines, and cook for 3–5 minutes. Strain the fish and vegetables and arrange in a large, warmed serving dish.

6 Reduce the sauce by boiling rapidly for 10 minutes. Check the seasoning and pour over the fish and vegetables. Serve with the croûtons and the rouille. You can spread the rouille on the croûtons or drop a dollop into the fish dish.

FAT: 44G (67%) • PROTEIN: 51G (102%) • CARBOHYDRATE: 28G (9%) • FIBER: 3G (13%)
VITAMIN C: 50% • MANGANESE: 186% • IRON: 35% • CHOLESTEROL: 39%

POULTRY

Honeyed Chicken with Passion Fruit

Poultry is an excellent source of protein—and full of flavor if you buy organic. It is rich in the B-complex vitamins, especially cholesterol-lowering B_3 (niacin), which also promotes healthy digestion and glowing skin, as well as boosting energy levels. The honey and the vitamin C will increase your resistance to disease. Finally, the potassium-packed passion fruit can help maintain a healthy heart.

SERVES 6

½ cup (80g) passion fruit pulp

6 organic chicken breasts, skinless

4 tbsp olive oil

juice of 3 lemons

2 tsp ground cinnamon

4 tbsp honey

1in (2.5cm) fresh root ginger, grated

freshly ground black pepper

4 cups (300g) arugula leaves

1 To pulp the passion fruits, cut them in half and scoop out the flesh. Mix together the olive oil, lemon juice, cinnamon, honey, and ginger to form a marinade. Coat the chicken breasts in the marinade. Season, and chill for 2 hours.

2 Drain the marinade from the chicken and cook the meat on a griddle pan, over a high heat, for 2 minutes on each side.

3 Put the chicken breasts on a baking sheet, cover with the passion fruit pulp, and finish cooking in a preheated oven (375°F/190°C/Gas 5) for 8 minutes. Serve on a bed of arugula leaves, which provide plenty of iron and vitamins.

FAT: 16G (25%) • PROTEIN: 59G (118%) • CARBOHYDRATE: 20G (7%) • FIBER: 4G (16%)
VITAMIN A: 140% • VITAMIN B$_3$: 216% • VITAMIN C: 40% • IRON: 25% • POTASSIUM: 81% • CHOLESTEROL: 52%

Chicken Jambalaya

The best known of the carotenoids is betacarotene. The body converts this to vitamin A, which is vital for new cell growth. It can also improve skin condition, especially in cases of acne, and can help slow the aging process. So if you want to look as young as you feel, then this recipe, with its Spanish origins and high betacarotene content, is the dish for you. Its high potassium levels will help to reduce blood pressure and counter the high-fat content of the chorizo sausage.

SERVES 6

4 tbsp olive oil

1 large onion, diced

6 garlic cloves, chopped

1 green pepper, diced

2 red chilies, deseeded and chopped

½ cup (100g) celery, chopped

9oz (250g) smoked chorizo sausage, sliced

2lb 4oz (1kg) chicken pieces, boneless and skinless

2 bay leaves

2 sprigs of fresh thyme, chopped

1 generous pinch of Spanish cayenne pepper

freshly ground black pepper

1lb 2oz (500g) white rice

4¾ cups (1.2 liters) chicken stock

2 tomatoes, chopped

3 tbsp chopped fresh parsley

1 Heat the olive oil in a large, flat-bottomed pan. Cook the onion, garlic, green pepper, red chilies, celery, and chorizo for 5 minutes. Add the chicken pieces, bay leaves, thyme, cayenne pepper, and seasoning.

2 Cook until all the chicken pieces are beginning to brown, then add the rice and stir for 2 minutes until all the grains are thoroughly coated.

3 Pour in the chicken stock and add the tomatoes and fresh parsley. Cook for 20 minutes until all the liquid has been completely absorbed. Serve with brown rice and a salad.

FAT: 41G (63%) • PROTEIN: 56G (112%) • CARBOHYDRATE: 34G (11%)
FIBER: 2G (10%) • VITAMIN A: 50% • VITAMIN C: 140% • POTASSIUM: 91%
CHOLESTEROL: 62%

Turkey and Green Bean Stir-Fry

The turkey in this dish is a low-fat option and provides vitamin D—the sunshine vitamin—which enables the body to use both calcium and phosphorous properly to make strong bones and teeth. The roasted sesame seeds provide vitamin B_3 (niacin), which keeps the heart and muscles functioning and helps to lift the spirits.

SERVES 6

2 tbsp sesame oil

14oz (400g) turkey breasts, skinless and cut widthways into thin strips

1½ cups (100g) oyster mushrooms, sliced

3 cups (150g) fresh bamboo shoots, diced

3 medium-sized carrots, thinly sliced diagonally

6 tbsp chicken stock

4 tbsp Japanese soy sauce

1 cup (125g) fresh green beans, sliced diagonally

4 tbsp sesame seeds, toasted

1 Heat the sesame oil in a wok and stir-fry the turkey strips for 2 minutes. Add the mushrooms, bamboo shoots, and carrots and cook for 3 minutes. Add the stock and soy sauce and cook for a further 20 minutes, until the carrots are tender but still firm.

2 Add the sliced green beans and roasted sesame seeds and cook for 5 more minutes, stirring continuously. Serve with fragrant white rice.

For variety, use bean sprouts, peas, or zucchini instead of the green beans.

FAT: 8G (12%) • PROTEIN: 24G (48%) • CARBOHYDRATE: 7G (2%)
FIBER: 3G (11%) • VITAMIN A: 140% • VITAMIN B_3: 51% • VITAMIN D: 4%
IRON: 15% • POTASSIUM: 50% • CHOLESTEROL: 18%

Chicken Kuroke (Japanese-Style Chicken Cakes)

The vitamin D in this recipe comes, surprisingly, from the immunity-boosting Japanese shiitake mushrooms, which have a proven antiviral action. They stop viruses from dividing and are thus said to protect against the flu. They are traditionally eaten to reduce fatigue and lower blood pressure, slow aging, and prevent ulcers.

SERVES 6 ① ④ ⑥ ⑧ ⑨ ⑩

3½oz (100g) fresh (or dried and rehydrated) shiitake mushrooms, sliced

1 garlic clove, sliced

4 scallions, chopped

5 tbsp olive oil

2 medium-sized fresh eggs, beaten

2 tbsp Japanese soy sauce

1½ cups (350g) mashed potatoes

1 cup (250g) leftover cooked chicken meat, finely chopped

½ cup (100g) breadcrumbs

1¾oz (50g) roasted Nori, crushed

1 Sauté the mushrooms, garlic, and scallions in 4 teaspoonfuls of the olive oil for 3 minutes. Let them cool.
2 In a large bowl, combine the mushroom mixture with the eggs, soy sauce, mashed potatoes, and chicken meat. From this mix, form even-sized balls and flatten them to shape eight small cakes.
3 Mix the breadcrumbs with the crushed Nori and roll the chicken cakes in this mixture. Cook them in a shallow pool of the remaining olive oil for about 5 minutes until they are golden and the centers are heated through. Serve on salad with a little soy sauce.

FAT: 13G (20%) • PROTEIN: 29G (58%) • CARBOHYDRATE: 42G (14%)
FIBER: 3G (13%) • VITAMIN D: 52% • CALCIUM: 15% • IRON: 20% • CHOLESTEROL: 74%

Spiedini di Pollo

This dish has a great name and wonderful health benefits. Surveys have found a direct relationship between selenium levels and cancer rates—the higher the former, the lower the latter. The Cancer Institute in the United States reckons that a protective daily dose of 200mcg of selenium could eventually see a 70 percent drop in rates of all cancers. Bread was always an excellent source of selenium, but thanks to overrefining, most varieties no longer contain it, with the result that much of the population is now deficient in this important antioxidant mineral.

SERVES 4

4 chicken breasts, skinless

juice of 3 lemons

4 tbsp olive oil

1 pinch of cayenne pepper

2 bay leaves

1 sprig of fresh thyme, chopped

16 baby white onions, peeled

24 large fresh sage leaves

24 slices of smoked pancetta

16 lemon wedges

(you will also need 8 metal skewers for cooking)

1 Cut each chicken breast into six pieces. Combine the lemon juice, olive oil, cayenne pepper, bay leaves, thyme, and whole onions in a bowl to make a marinade. Add the pieces of meat and leave to chill in the refrigerator for 3–4 hours.
2 Remove the chicken from the marinade, reserving the onions for later. Roll a large sage leaf around each piece of marinated chicken. Then carefully wrap each bundle in a slice of pancetta.
3 On a skewer, thread a lemon wedge, skin first, followed by a baby onion, three chicken and pancetta bundles, another baby onion, and a last lemon wedge, flesh first. Do the same for the remaining seven skewers.
4 To cook, broil or barbecue for 20–25 minutes, turning frequently. Serve two skewers per person with salad or pasta.

FAT: 22G (34%) • PROTEIN: 48G (96%) • CARBOHYDRATE: 23G (8%)
FIBER: 8G (31%) • CALCIUM: 30% • IRON: 35% • SELENIUM: 20% • CHOLESTEROL: 41%

Chicken Marengo

Chicken is a rich source of magnesium, which is known as the antistress mineral. It converts blood sugar into energy and plays a vital role in nerve and muscle function. It can also help fight depression, protect against heart attacks, aid digestion, and keep tooth enamel safe from decay. Heavy drinking lowers levels of this mineral in the body.

SERVES 6

4 tbsp olive oil

freshly ground black pepper

1 large whole chicken (about 6lb/2.7kg), cut into 8 pieces and skinned

1 large onion, chopped

5 garlic cloves, crushed

4 cups (400g) button mushrooms, sliced

2 tomatoes, skinned, deseeded, and chopped

½ cup (125ml) white wine

1 sprig of fresh thyme

1 bay leaf

2 tbsp fresh flat-leaf parsley, chopped, to garnish

1 Heat the olive oil in a large, heavy-based pan. Season the chicken pieces and cook until brown. Remove the meat and put to one side.
2 Cook the onion and garlic in the chicken juices, until they soften. Then add the mushrooms, tomatoes, wine, thyme, and bay leaves.
3 Return the chicken pieces to the pan, cover and cook for 1 hour over a low heat. Sprinkle with the chopped parsley before serving.

FAT: 29G (44%) • PROTEIN: 143G (286%) • CARBOHYDRATE: 10G (3%) • FIBER: 3G (11%)
VITAMIN C: 45% • MAGNESIUM: 48% • IRON: 40% • CHOLESTEROL: 129%

Chicken Provençale

This recipe contains the three big powerful antioxidant vitamins A, C, and E. The vitamins A and C come from the red peppers. Vitamin E, which enhances the activity of both vitamins A and C, is provided by the olive oil. Unlike other fat-soluble vitamins, vitamin E—which repairs tissue and reduces blood pressure—is stored in the body for only a short time, so it is important to eat it every day.

SERVES 6

3lb 6oz (1.5kg) chicken legs and thighs, skinless

6 tbsp olive oil

2 large onions, chopped

5 garlic cloves, chopped

3 large shallots, chopped

6 red peppers, cut into thick strips

4 tomatoes, chopped

½ cup (125ml) white wine

1 sprig of fresh oregano

1 sprig of fresh thyme

2 bay leaves, crushed

1 pinch of cayenne pepper

freshly ground black pepper

¾ cup (150g) pitted green olives

½ cup (100g) pitted black olives

5 fresh basil leaves, chopped

1 Brown the chicken pieces in olive oil for 5 minutes, remove from the pan, and put to one side.
2 In the same pan, gently cook the onions, garlic, and shallots until tender. Then add the red pepper strips, chopped tomatoes, wine, oregano, thyme, bay leaves, and cayenne pepper.
3 Next, return the chicken pieces to the pan. Season, cover, and cook very slowly for 1 hour over a low heat.
4 Add the olives and cook for another 20 minutes before sprinkling with chopped fresh basil and serving hot with rice or fresh pasta.

FAT: 39G (60%) • PROTEIN: 55G (110%) • CARBOHYDRATE: 23G (8%)
FIBER: 4G (16%) • VITAMIN A: 80% • VITAMIN C: 270% • VITAMIN E: 34%
CHOLESTEROL: 61%

Chicken Moorg

The B vitamins work better in combination than they do alone and poultry combined with brown rice provide most of them. The chicken contains vitamin B_3 (niacin), which can help to lower cholesterol and blood pressure, regulate sex hormones, and improve skin condition; vitamin B_6, which is believed to play a role in the synthesis of antiaging nucleic acids; and vitamin B_{12}, which is known as the red vitamin because it helps to build healthy blood.

SERVES 6　

1 large onion, chopped

6 garlic cloves, chopped

1in (2.5cm) fresh root ginger, grated

juice of 2 lemons

6 chicken legs, skinned

3 chicken breasts, skinned

¼ tsp ground cinnamon

¼ tsp freshly grated nutmeg

¼ tsp cloves

¼ tsp mace

1 tsp ground cumin

1 tsp ground turmeric

1 tsp ground coriander

¼ tsp cayenne pepper

6 tbsp olive oil

1 cup (250ml) low-fat natural yogurt

2 tbsp fresh cilantro, chopped, to garnish

For the brown pilau rice:

1 large onion

4 tsp olive oil

1 piece of cinnamon stick

2 cups (450g) brown rice

4 cups (1 liter) vegetable stock

1 Put the chopped onion, garlic, ginger, and lemon juice in a food processor and blend to a very smooth paste. Add the dry spices, olive oil, and yogurt. These then form the marinade.

2 Slash the legs and the breast of the chicken pieces and place them in a large bowl. Rub the marinade over the chicken pieces, cover, and leave them to rest in the refrigerator for 24 hours.

3 Wrap the chicken and marinade in foil and cook on a baking sheet for 1½ hours in a preheated oven (400°F/200°C/Gas 6). Baste the meat with the marinade during cooking.

4 To make the brown pilau rice, sweat the onion in the olive oil with the cinnamon stick for 5–6 minutes until translucent. Add the rice and stir for 2 minutes to coat every grain.

5 Pour in the vegetable stock, then bring the mixture to the boil. Pour into an ovenproof casserole dish, cover, and cook in a preheated oven (350°F/180°C/Gas 4) for 25–30 minutes. Garnish the chicken with fresh cilantro and serve with the pilau rice.

FAT: 11G (16%) • PROTEIN: 46G (92%) • CARBOHYDRATE: 28G (9%) • FIBER: 3G (11%)
VITAMIN B_3: 135% • VITAMIN B_6: 58% • VITAMIN B_{12}: 23% • CHOLESTEROL: 41%

MEAT

Tajine

The apricots in this delicious, protein-rich North African stew are an outstanding source of both iron and betacarotene, which the body converts to vitamin A. Everyone knows that you need iron to make red blood cells, but it is less well known that women, who in one month lose almost twice as much iron as men, are frequently borderline anemic. This dish will prevent this.

SERVES 6

3 large onions, chopped

1lb 12oz (800g) pork (shoulder), diced

1lb 12oz (800g) lamb (middle neck), diced

4 tbsp olive oil

4 tsp cumin seeds

2 tbsp coriander seeds

1 cinnamon stick

1 pinch of cayenne pepper

4 cups (1 liter) chicken stock

6 carrots, sliced

juice of two lemons

⅔ cup (80g) blanched almonds

8 dried apricots

4 tsp honey

1 tbsp fresh cilantro, roughly chopped, to garnish

1 Put the chopped onions, diced meats, oil, cumin, coriander seeds, cinnamon stick, and cayenne pepper in an ovenproof dish with a lid. Cover with chicken stock (or water) and cook, covered, in a preheated oven (375°F/190°C/Gas 5) for 2 hours.

2 Add the sliced carrots, lemon juice, blanched almonds, and dried apricots and return to the oven for another 1½ hours.

3 Uncover the tajine, stir the honey into the cooking juices, and return to the oven to cook until the sauce has thickened (about 20 minutes). Serve very hot in its cooking pot, garnished with some roughly chopped cilantro.

You can make tajine with lamb, pork, or beef if you prefer. It is delicious served with couscous, another traditional North African dish.

FAT: 51G (79%) • PROTEIN: 64G (128%) • CARBOHYDRATE: 23G (8%) • FIBER: 7G (29%)
VITAMIN A: 270% • IRON: 45% • MAGNESIUM: 47% • CHOLESTEROL: 72%

Fillet of Pork with Prunes

Pork and prunes are a delicious taste combination. What's more, this is a very healthy dish. The prunes contain potassium, which promotes the efficient disposal of the body's waste products and is needed in large quantities by people with diabetes, high blood pressure and liver disease. Pork is rich in vitamin B_3 (niacin), which is always depleted by stress, illness, or surgery.

SERVES 6

18 prunes

2lb 4oz (1kg) pork fillet

⅔ cup (90g) walnuts

⅔ cup (90g) almonds

⅔ cup (90g) hazelnuts

⅓ cup (100ml) honey

4 tbsp cider vinegar

1¼ cups (300ml) chicken stock

freshly ground black pepper

⅓ cup (50g) white flour (for coating the pork)

4 tbsp olive oil

1 bunch of fresh chives, chopped, to garnish

1 Soak the prunes in water for 8 hours. Trim the pork fillets and cut, widthways, into 1in (2.5cm) disks. Gently crush the nuts. Drain the prunes and cut them in half.

2 In a pan, heat the honey until it turns to a caramel color. Add the vinegar with the chicken stock. Season and reduce the sauce until it becomes syrupy and coats the back of a spoon. Complete the sauce by adding the nuts and the prunes. Put to one side.

3 Coat each piece of pork in flour and brown in hot olive oil until golden on both sides. Allow 4 minutes cooking time on each side. Season and serve. Present the pork covered with the prune sauce and garnished with chopped chives. Serve with a selection of vegetables.

FAT: 51G (79%) • PROTEIN: 41G (82%) • CARBOHYDRATE: 44G (15%)
FIBER: 6G (24%) • VITAMIN B₃: 79% • VITAMIN E: 59%
POTASSIUM: 117% • CHOLESTEROL: 35%

Pork with Tofu and Vegetables

This recipe provides 71.44mg of vitamin C per serving—the intake for optimum health is between 60 and 100mcg. In mega doses—around 5,000mg a day—vitamin C becomes a medicine that has been shown to lengthen life expectancy of patients diagnosed with terminal cancer. Tofu is an amazing food that contains powerful phytochemicals, which many now believe can actually reverse diseases, including cancers and heart disease.

SERVES 6

1lb 11oz (750g) lean pork, cut into 2.5cm (1in) cubes

½ cup (100g) chopped celery

3½oz (100g) bamboo shoots, sliced

1 large onion, sliced in rings

2 cups (250ml) tofu, cut into 1in (2.5cm) cubes

1 Chinese cabbage, chopped into squares

3½oz (100g) spinach leaves

For the Asian-style sauce:

½ cup (125ml) soy sauce

juice of 2 lemons

4 tsp rice vinegar

1in (2.5cm) piece fresh root ginger, grated

1 scallion, chopped

1 Place the pork in a pan and cover with water. Cook for 40 minutes, skimming the top while cooking. Add the celery, sliced bamboo shoots, onion slices, tofu, cabbage, and spinach to the pork and cook for another 20–30 minutes.

2 Combine all the ingredients for the sauce in a small bowl and mix together well.

3 Bring the pork with its stock and the vegetables directly to the table in a large pot. Serve with white rice and the Asian-style sauce.

FAT: 17G (27%) • PROTEIN: 32G (64%) • CARBOHYDRATE: 8G (3%)
FIBER: 3G (11%) • VITAMIN A: 100% • VITAMIN C: 120% • FOLIC ACID: 35%
CHOLESTEROL: 26%

Nepalese Pork Curry

Vitamin C is a multirole nutrient—it improves the body's ability to absorb other vitamins and minerals, especially calcium and iron, and helps flush out toxic metals such as mercury and lead. In this dish, the high levels come from the red pepper. However, vitamin C does not stay in the body for long—eat it at breakfast and it is gone from the body by noon. Most meat dishes are high in saturated fats, which can increase cholesterol levels. Thanks to the trimmed pork, this dish is one of the healthier meat options.

SERVES 6

1lb 12 oz (800g) boneless pork	**1 green pepper, sliced**
3 onions, finely chopped	**1 red pepper, sliced**
5 garlic cloves, finely chopped	**1 cup (250ml) water**
4 tbsp olive oil	**1 cup (250ml) natural yogurt**
1 tsp ground coriander	**freshly ground black pepper**
1 tsp ground cumin	**4 tbsp fresh chives, chopped**
½ tsp chili powder	

1 Trim the fat from the pork and cut into average-sized pieces. In an ovenproof casserole dish, cook the onion and garlic in the olive oil for 5 minutes, stirring constantly.
2 Add the coriander, cumin, and chili and cook for another 2 minutes. Now add the pork pieces and stir until they are coated with the spices. Add the sliced peppers, water, and yogurt. Season to taste.
3 bring to a boil on the hob and then cook in a preheated oven (350°F/180°C/Gas 4) for 1½ hours, until the meat is tender. Sprinkle with the chopped chives and serve with nutty Italian brown rice.

FAT: 26G (40%) • PROTEIN: 29G (58%) • CARBOHYDRATE: 11G (4%)
FIBER: 3G (10%) • VITAMIN A: 45% • VITAMIN B₃: 55% • VITAMIN C: 140%
CHOLESTEROL: 29%

Thai Green Beef Curry

If you eat meat, enjoy this high-fat dish as an occasional treat. Although it is higher in saturated fats (33g per portion) than any other recipe in this book, most of the fat comes from the coconut milk, rather than from the beef. As well as imparting the traditional Thai flavor, coconut milk is packed with nutrients: it provides more carbohydrate, fiber, vitamin E, folic acid, calcium, copper, selenium, magnesium, and manganese than any other single ingredient in this dish.

SERVES 4

1lb 5oz (600g) best lean beef fillet, cut into strips	*For the green curry paste:*
2 cups (500ml) coconut milk	**1 fresh green chili**
1 red chili, deseeded and chopped	**2 tbsp fresh cilantro**
1½in (4cm) piece fresh root ginger, grated	**1 onion, diced**
3 kaffir lime leaves	**1 tbsp sesame oil**
2 tbsp Thai fish sauce	**½ tsp ground turmeric**
1 tbsp brown sugar	**½ tsp shrimp paste**
3 tbsp sesame oil, to fry	**1 garlic clove, crushed**
	1 lemon grass stalk, roughly chopped
	½ tsp ground cumin
	½ tsp caraway seeds

1 To make the green curry paste, blend all the ingredients in a food processor to form a smooth paste. Heat the oil in a wok and cook this paste for 1 minute.
2 Add the beef strips to the paste and stir-fry for 1 minute. Add the coconut milk, chili, ginger, kaffir lime leaves, fish sauce, and brown sugar. bring to a boil, stirring constantly. Cook for 8 minutes. Serve with white rice and noodles.

FAT: 49G (76%) • PROTEIN: 50G (100%) • CARBOHYDRATE: 15G (5%)
FIBER: 4G (16%) • VITAMIN B₃: 140% • VITAMIN C: 100% • VITAMIN E: 140%
CALCIUM: 10% • COPPER: 35% • FOLIC ACID: 10% • IRON: 50% • MAGNESIUM: 36%
MANGANESE: 53% • SELENIUM: 21% • CHOLESTEROL: 165%

Steak Teriyaki

One of the symptoms of vitamin B_{12} deficiency is extreme fatigue. If you are vegetarian, or are on a diet that excludes eggs and dairy products, you run the risk of this deficiency, which can take up to five years for the symptoms to manifest themselves. This recipe is an effective rejuvenator because it combines meat, a rich source of vitamin B_{12}, and sesame seeds, full of folic acid, which will give you a boost when you are feeling run down.

SERVES 4 ② ③ ④ ⑥

4 x 6¼oz (180g) beef fillet steaks	*For the marinade:*
1 cup (125g) whole-wheat noodles	½ cup (125ml) Japanese soy sauce
4 tsp olive oil	4 tsp sugar
2 tbsp sesame seeds, roasted	8 tsp sake
	2 garlic cloves, crushed
	1in (2.5cm) piece fresh root ginger, grated

1 Combine all the marinade ingredients in a bowl. Add the steaks and leave in the refrigerator to chill for at least 3 hours, turning the meat frequently.
2 Drain the fillets, reserving the marinade, and cook them on both sides on a nonstick griddle pan. Baste the meat with the marinade while cooking and, when done, put to one side.
3 Cook the noodles in boiling water for 3 minutes. Drain and toss with olive oil and sesame seeds. Slice the beef into very thin slices and serve with the noodles.

FAT: 27G (41%) • PROTEIN: 59G (118%) • CARBOHYDRATE: 26G (9%)
FIBER: 3G (12%) • VITAMIN B₁₂: 92% • FOLIC ACID: 6% • IRON: 45%
POTASSIUM: 99% • CHOLESTEROL: 50%

Costoletie d'Agnello al Parmigiano

Succulent spring lamb is an excellent source of phosphorous, the second most abundant mineral in the body. Most of it is in the bones and teeth where, together with calcium and fluoride, it makes the tissues hard. It is crucial to the formation of phospholipids, which regulate what goes in and out of cells and which are vital to both the release and storage of energy.

SERVES 4 ③ ⑤ ⑥

2 racks of lamb, trimmed	*For the Parmesan crust:*
4 tbsp olive oil	10 black olives, pitted
2 bay leaves	10 fresh sage leaves
3 sprigs of fresh rosemary	½ cup (100g) fresh Parmesan, grated
1 sprig of fresh thyme	4 tbsp olive oil
	5 garlic cloves, crushed

1 To make the Parmesan crust, put all the ingredients in a food processor and blend for 1 minute.
2 Seal the racks of lamb by frying them quickly over a high heat in olive oil, with the bay leaves, rosemary, and thyme, until they have browned all over.
3 Place the meat in an ovenproof dish and cover with the Parmesan crust paste. Cook in a preheated oven (350°F/180°C/Gas 4) for 20 minutes. When the meat is cooked, cover and leave to rest for 15 minutes. Cut the chops and serve with Swiss Chard—Two Ways *(see page 106)*.

FAT: 59G (91%) • PROTEIN: 63G (126%) • CARBOHYDRATE: 4G (1%)
FIBER: 0.56G (2%) • CALCIUM: 40% • PHOSPHOROUS: 75% • SELENIUM: 118%
CHOLESTEROL: 65%

Beef Kebab with Moroccan Sauce and Bulgur Wheat

If you love meat, hate vegetables, and can't be bothered to spend hours in the kitchen cooking, this is the dish for you. Not least because you can cook it outdoors. Rich in all the B vitamins, potassium, and zinc from the meat, it is also packed with fiber from the bulgur wheat, polyunsaturated fat from the pine nuts, and vitamins A and C from the red onions, chilies, and tomatoes.

SERVES 6

2 red onions, finely diced

3 red chilies, deseeded and finely diced

3 tbsp chopped fresh mint

1 tsp chopped fresh thyme

4 tsp olive oil

1 tsp ground cumin

1in (2.5cm) piece fresh root ginger, grated

½ tsp Tabasco sauce

freshly ground black pepper

1 cup (200g) bulgur wheat

2 cups (500ml) chicken stock

3 tbsp chopped fresh flat-leaf parsley

2lb 4oz (1kg) lean beef, minced

1 white onion, finely diced

For the Moroccan sauce:

1 small onion, diced

5 tsp olive oil

2 tomatoes, skinned, deseeded and chopped

1 tsp ground cumin

4 tbsp pine kernels, roasted

½ cup (80g) raisins

(you will also need 6 kebab skewers)

1 Put the red onion and chilies in a bowl with the fresh mint, thyme, olive oil, cumin, ginger, and Tabasco sauce, reserving a little of the mint for garnish. Season, mix well, and leave to chill for at least 2 hours in the refrigerator.

2 Meanwhile, put the bulgur wheat in a large pot. Add the chicken stock and diced white onion, season, and cook until the wheat has absorbed all the stock. When cooked, add the chopped parsley and put to one side.

3 To make the Moroccan sauce, cook the onion in olive oil, until tender. Add the tomatoes, cumin, pine kernels, and raisins. Season and leave to cook gently over a low heat for 20 minutes.

4 To make the kebabs, roll the meat around the skewer, making a long sausage shape from one end to the other. Broil or barbecue for 6–8 minutes, turning all the time to ensure even cooking.

5 Serve the beef kebabs on a bed of herbed bulgur wheat, surrounded by the sauce and garnished with a sprinkle of fresh mint.

As a variation, serve the kebabs with couscous or rice.

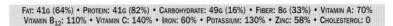

FAT: 41G (64%) • PROTEIN: 41G (82%) • CARBOHYDRATE: 49G (16%) • FIBER: 8G (33%) • VITAMIN A: 70% VITAMIN B$_{12}$: 110% • VITAMIN C: 140% • IRON: 60% • POTASSIUM: 130% • ZINC: 58% • CHOLESTEROL: 0

Gratinée of Pumpkin in its Shell

Crammed with goodness, this is practically the perfect healthy dish. Several of its nutrients either reach or surpass the minimum recommended daily amounts and its high levels of vitamins A and C pack a powerful anticancer punch. Pumpkin seeds are an excellent source of zinc, which, as well as being an antioxidant in its own right, aids the absorption of cancer-fighting vitamin A. Among its many health benefits, zinc also helps to strengthen the immune system, promote reproductive health, and protect the prostate.

SERVES 4   ② ③ ④ ⑤ ⑥ ⑦ ⑧ ⑨ ⑩

1 large pumpkin

4 tsp olive oil

1 large onion, diced

9 slices mixed grain bread, cubed

4 tbsp pumpkin seeds, broiled

4 tbsp sunflower seeds, broiled

¾ cup (150g) Gruyère cheese, grated

¾ cup (150g) low-fat, low-sodium hard cheese, grated

1 bunch of fresh chervil, chopped

4 cups (1 liter) soy milk

1 tsp allspice

freshly ground black pepper

1 Create a kind of soup tureen with the pumpkin by slicing off the top to form a lid, which you are going to replace. Scoop out the seeds and the flesh, without piercing the skin. Dice the flesh. Heat the olive oil until very hot and then cook the pumpkin flesh with the onion until tender.

2 Inside the pumpkin shell, place alternate layers of cubed bread, cooked pumpkin flesh, pumpkin and sunflower seeds, the two cheeses, and the chervil, finishing with a cheese layer on the top. Reserve a little cheese for a garnish.

3 Whisk the soy milk and allspice together. Season and pour into the pumpkin. Cover with its own lid, wrap carefully in foil and cook in a preheated oven (275°F/140°C/Gas 1) for 2 hours. Serve garnished with chopped chervil.

FAT: 40G (62%) • PROTEIN: 48G (96%) • CARBOHYDRATE: 89G (39%) • FIBER: 13G (54%)
VITAMIN A: 240% • VITAMIN C: 110% • CALCIUM: 90% • IRON: 70% • ZINC: 52% • CHOLESTEROL: 16%

VEGETABLES

Broccoli and Almond Risotto

Eating more vegetables will dramatically reduce your risk of disease, but if you really want to swing the odds in favor of a long and healthy life, then you need to eat the right vegetables. You should definitely eat more broccoli: it lowers the risk of cancer—especially of the colon, lung, and prostate—and has been shown to block the cell mutations that foreshadow any cancer. For optimum health, eat broccoli three times a week.

SERVES 6

1 head of broccoli

1 red onion, finely diced

1 garlic clove, chopped

6 tbsp olive oil

1½ cups (300g) Arborio rice

4 cups (1 liter) vegetable stock

6 fresh sage leaves, sliced

freshly ground black pepper

4 tbsp almond cream

½ cup (100g) blanched almonds

4 tbsp fresh Parmesan cheese, grated, plus extra shavings to garnish

1 Blanch (cook briefly) the broccoli in a pan of boiling water. In another large pan, cook the diced onion and chopped garlic in the olive oil until tender (do not let them discolor).

2 Add the rice and stir for 2 minutes to coat all the grains. Cover the rice with a little of the hot vegetable stock and cook gently for 10 minutes, stirring frequently.

3 Add the broccoli, sage, and seasoning. Gradually add more stock as the rice absorbs all the liquid. Continue to cook until the rice is tender (it should take approximately 25 minutes in total).

4 When the rice is cooked, add the almond cream, whole almonds, and Parmesan cheese and stir. Check the seasoning and, just before serving, sprinkle the risotto with Parmesan shavings.

As a variation, use other nuts or different blanched vegetables, for example asparagus or green beans.

FAT: 25G (38%) • PROTEIN: 12G (24%) • CARBOHYDRATE: 49G (16%)
FIBER: 5G (18%) • VITAMIN E: 48% • CALCIUM: 20% • POTASSIUM: 33%
CHOLESTEROL: 2%

Cilantro Potato Bake

Potatoes are high in silica, which is essential for the body's connective tissues, especially lung tissue, which it helps to keep elastic. In healthy people the *Solanaceae* family of vegetables (which includes potatoes) can stop calcium deposits from building up. This dish also contains cilantro, which has potent antifungal and antibacterial properties (the Romans used it to preserve meats) and is good for both the circulation and the digestive system. Cilantro is also an aphrodisiac, so if you're planning a candlelit seduction, serve this dish as your main course.

SERVES 4

6 tbsp tomato purée

1 cup (250ml) vegetable stock

7 large potatoes, diced

2 tbsp paprika

8 garlic cloves, chopped

2 tbsp chopped fresh cilantro

freshly ground black pepper

4 tbsp olive oil

1 Mix the tomato purée into the vegetable stock. Put the potatoes, paprika, vegetable stock, garlic, and chopped cilantro into an ovenproof dish, reserving some of the cilantro for a garnish. Add the olive oil for flavor.

2 Mix everything together, season, cover, and cook in a preheated oven (325°F/170°C/Gas 3) for 1 hour until the potatoes are soft. Check the seasoning and garnish with fresh cilantro before serving.

FAT: 13G (20%) • PROTEIN: 9G (18%) • CARBOHYDRATE: 65G (22%)
FIBER: 8G (32%) • VITAMIN A: 120% • VITAMIN C: 120% • VITAMIN E: 16%
CHOLESTEROL: 0

Imam Bayildi (Turkish Stuffed Eggplants)

This cholesterol-free Turkish dish is packed with potassium, which unites with phosphorous to send oxygen to the brain. Potassium keeps blood pressure stable and skin healthy and is critical to the synthesis of protein and nucleic acids. Eggplants help maintain lower blood cholesterol, prevent plaque building up in the arteries, and have both antibacterial and diuretic properties.

SERVES 6　　　　　3 4 6 7 9 10

1½ cups (200g) raisins	**10 tomatoes, skinned, deseeded, and chopped**
6 eggplants	
juice of 2 lemons	**5 garlic cloves, crushed**
½ cup (125ml) olive oil	**1 pinch of cayenne pepper**
5 large onions, finely chopped	**1 sprig of fresh thyme**
	3 bay leaves
5 tbsp chopped fresh flat-leaf parsley	**freshly ground black pepper**

1 Soak the raisins in a bowl of warm water. Halve the eggplants lengthwise. Extract and dice the flesh without piercing the skins. Mix the flesh with the juice of 1 lemon.
2 Heat the olive oil and sauté the diced eggplants, onions, parsley, tomatoes, crushed garlic, cayenne pepper, thyme, and bay leaves. Season and cook for 30 minutes. Drain the raisins and add to this mixture when cooked.
3 Place the empty eggplant skins in an ovenproof dish. Stuff them with the vegetable mixture and cook in a preheated oven (325°F/160°C/Gas 3) for 1½ hours. Squeeze over the juice of the second lemon before serving.

To make this a meat dish, add 10½oz (300g) of lean minced lamb to the stuffing with the raisins.

Avoid eggplant if you suffer from arthritis.

FAT: 17G (27%) • PROTEIN: 10G (20%) • CARBOHYDRATE: 78G (26%)
FIBER: 19G (77%) • VITAMIN C: 120% • POTASSIUM: 229% • CHOLESTEROL: 0

Summer Tabbouleh

A diet that is high in antioxidant-rich tomatoes is linked with low rates of both pancreatic and cervical cancer. Tomatoes are the best source of lycopene—a lesser known carotenoid that researchers now believe is a more potent antioxidant than betacarotene. Blood levels of lycopene drop with age and if you are over 50 and do not suffer from arthritis, you should try to eat a tomato or tomato product a day.

SERVES 6　　　　　 2 3 4 6 7 8

1 cucumber	**6 tbsp chopped fresh parsley**
5 cups (500g) bulgur wheat	
juice of 3 lemons	**4 tbsp chopped fresh cilantro**
½ cup (125ml) olive oil	**3 tbsp chopped fresh mint**
4 ripe beef tomatoes, skinned, deseeded, and chopped	**1 large onion, thinly sliced**
	freshly ground black pepper

1 Peel the cucumber and slice it in half. Scrape out the seeds with a teaspoon and cut the flesh into small cubes.
2 Cook the bulgur wheat in boiling water for 15 minutes until tender. Strain the wheat and leave to rest. When the wheat is cold, add the lemon juice, olive oil, tomatoes, parsley, cilantro, mint, sliced onion, cucumber, and seasoning. Chill for at least 2 hours before serving.

For a change, you can make this dish with couscous. For the best results, make the tabbouleh 24 hours before you want to serve it.

FAT: 17G (26%) • PROTEIN: 13G (26%) • CARBOHYDRATE: 68G (23%)
FIBER: 11G (45%) • VITAMIN C: 35% • MAGNESIUM: 45%
POTASSIUM: 69% • CHOLESTEROL: 0

Spinach and Goats' Cheese Lasagna

It gave Popeye his muscles, but spinach is actually more likely to lower levels of homocysteine, a blood protein that is now recognized as a major indicator of heart disease. Spinach also prevents premature aging, protects eyesight, boosts immunity, and gives you strong bones and teeth. Spinach contains vitamin A which, as well as fighting cancer, supports the body's natural defenses and helps to regulate hormones. The nuts in this recipe contain vitamin E, which is said to slow down the aging process.

SERVES 4

10 cups (500g) fresh spinach

¼ tsp freshly grated nutmeg

½ cup (50g) mixed nuts, including pecans, walnuts, hazelnuts, and brazil nuts, all finely chopped

½ tsp ground coriander

6 tbsp soy spread

6 tbsp all-purpose flour (use wheat-free if you have allergies)

2½ cups (600ml) soy milk

⅞ cup (200g) organic soft goats' cheese

½ tsp English mustard

freshly ground black pepper

1½ cups (175g) whole-wheat lasagne (use corn pasta if avoiding wheat)

paprika, to garnish

1 Cook the spinach in a large pot with a little water until it goes limp. Grate in the nutmeg and stir in the chopped nuts and the ground coriander.

2 In a small pan, make a bechamel sauce: gently melt the soy spread, add the flour, and cook for 2 minutes, stirring all the time. Add the soy milk gradually and bring to a boil, again stirring constantly. Simmer gently for a few more minutes until the sauce thickens.

3 Melt the goats' cheese into the sauce, keeping some back to sprinkle on the top of the finished dish. Stir in the mustard and season to taste.

4 Layer the spinach and nut mixture with the sheets of lasagne in an ovenproof dish. Pour the goats' cheese sauce over the top and sprinkle the last layer with the reserved cheese and paprika.

5 Bake at the top of a preheated oven (375°F/190°C/Gas 5) for 30 minutes and serve piping hot with crusty bread and a green salad.

FAT: 29G (44%) • PROTEIN: 23G (46%) • CARBOHYDRATE: 30G (10%)
FIBER: 8G (32%) • VITAMIN A: 190% • VITAMIN E: 39% • FOLATE: 69%
CHOLESTEROL: 8%

Parsnip and Horseradish Mash

Parsnips are frequently underrated. As well as tasting delicious, they have important health benefits. They contain more soluble fiber than any other everyday vegetable, helping to lower cholesterol, reduce blood pressure, and sweep cancer-causing agents through the colon and out of the body. Parsnips also contain six different types of anticancer agents. The horseradish in this tasty dish is a decongestant that loosens mucus, helping to clear respiratory disorders, including asthma and bronchitis. It also speeds up the metabolism slightly to burn more calories.

SERVES 4

2 potatoes, cut into chunks

8 parsnips, cut into chunks

⅞ cup (200ml) soy cream

⅔ cup (150ml) olive oil

3 tsp fresh horseradish, grated

1 pinch of freshly grated nutmeg

freshly ground black pepper

1 Cook the potatoes and parsnips together until soft. Heat up the soy cream.

2 Drain the vegetables and mash with the hot soy cream, slowly drizzling the olive oil into the pot as you mash. Add the remaining ingredients, season, and serve.

As an alternative, make the same dish with rutabagas or turnips instead of parsnips.

FAT: 40G (62%) • PROTEIN: 4G (8%) • CARBOHYDRATE: 54G (18%)
FIBER: 9G (35%) • VITAMIN C: 70% • POTASSIUM: 125% • CHOLESTEROL: 0

Cauliflower and Roquefort Fricassée

Walnuts are a concentrated source of omega-3 essential acids, which can lower high cholesterol and high blood pressure, reduce elevated blood tryglyceride levels, and help prevent blood clots. Even better, they can lower high levels of the protein homocysteine, which are now reckoned to be an even better indicator of a risk of heart problems than cholesterol. Walnuts are a good alternative to oily fish (also rich in omega-3 fatty acids) if you are vegetarian or are worried about eating fish that contains environmental toxins.

SERVES 4

1 large head of cauliflower, cut into florets	**½ cup (100g) black grapes, halved**
2 cups (300g) celery stalks, sliced	**½ cup (50g) walnuts**
½ lemon	**freshly ground black pepper**
3 tbsp olive oil	**⅔ cup (150ml) vegetable stock**
4 tbsp chopped fresh parsley	**½ cup (125g) Roquefort cheese, diced**

1 Blanch (cook briefly) the cauliflower florets, together with the celery and the lemon, in boiling water. (The lemon keeps the cauliflower white.) Drain well, discard the lemon, and sauté the cauliflower and celery in olive oil until they start to brown.

2 Add the parsley, grape halves, and walnuts. Season and cook for 5–7 minutes. Transfer this mix to a gratin dish. Heat the stock to boiling. Add to the dish and sprinkle the diced Roquefort over the top.

3 Bake in a preheated oven (350°F/180°C/Gas 4) for 20 minutes. Serve piping hot with a baby spinach salad on the side.

For variety, try this dish with Stilton or your own favorite blue cheese.

> FAT: 26G (41%) • PROTEIN: 14G (28%) • CARBOHYDRATE: 22G (7%)
> FIBER: 7G (28%) • VITAMIN C: 250% • CALCIUM: 30%
> OMEGA-3 FATTY ACIDS: 37% • CHOLESTEROL: 9%

Black-Eyed Bean Balti

This potassium-rich curry will boost energy levels and help maintain a healthy heart and circulation. Ginger is native to India, where it is used in traditional Ayurvedic medicine as a spiritual cleanser, and as a digestive aid. Ginger has many health benefits: it is an excellent antidepressant, and it boosts the immune system, warding off colds and the flu. Ginger also quells both motion and morning sickness and is used in some cultures to help treat impotence.

SERVES 4

1½ cups (300g) black-eyed beans	**3 tbsp olive oil**
4 bay leaves	**1 tsp ground cumin**
3 cardamom pods	**½ cup (125ml) low-fat natural yogurt**
3 garlic cloves, crushed	**3 sprigs of fresh cilantro, chopped, to garnish**
½ tsp ground turmeric	**3 onions, finely chopped**
1in (2.5cm) piece fresh root ginger, grated	**4 tomatoes**
2 dried red chilies, deseeded and crushed	

1 Soak the beans for 12 hours in cold water. Cook them slowly for 1 hour in boiling water with the bay leaves, cardamom, half the crushed garlic, and the turmeric until tender. When cooked, drain and reserve the liquid.

2 In a balti dish or a large, heavy-based pot, cook the onions, tomatoes, ginger, remaining garlic, and chilies in olive oil for 5 minutes. Add the ground cumin, black-eyed beans, yogurt, and some of the reserved liquid.

3 Cook for another 5 minutes until the sauce thickens. Garnish with fresh, chopped cilantro and serve with rice or chapatis.

> FAT: 11G (17%) • PROTEIN: 11G (22%) • CARBOHYDRATE: 38G (13%)
> FIBER: 10G (40%) • VITAMIN C: 60% • FOLATE: 37% • POTASSIUM: 93%
> CHOLESTEROL: 0

Country Bean and Lentil Pie

Never underestimate the humble bean, which provides colon-cleansing fiber, energy-boosting iron, and heart-protecting folate. In this dish, the often over-looked red kidney bean reigns supreme and provides the calcium and iron that is lacking in so many overrefined diets. The lentil had a hippy image, but is now served in all the most fashionable restaurants in the world's capital cities. It is also an important ingredient in trendy fusion cuisine.

SERVES 6

3 small white onions, diced

2 garlic cloves, crushed

4 tbsp olive oil

1 medium-sized eggplant, cut into chunks

2 medium-sized carrots, cut into chunks

2 zucchini, cut into chunks

3½ cups (900ml) vegetable stock

2 large beef tomatoes, skinned, deseeded, and chopped

2 cups (400g) chickpeas, soaked and cooked

1 cup (150g) red lentils

2 cups (400g) red kidney beans, soaked and cooked

2 cups (400g) green beans soaked and cooked with sage leaves

1 tbsp sunflower seeds

2 tsp tomato purée

splash of Tabasco and soy sauce, to taste

freshly ground black pepper

half a dozen fresh sage leaves, roughly chopped

For the topping:

3 large potatoes, suitable for mashing, peeled and chopped

3 tbsp low-fat sour cream

½ cup (100g) Feta cheese

1 In a heavy-based pot, gently soften the onion and garlic in the olive oil. Add the chunky chopped vegetables (eggplant, carrots, zucchini) and cook gently until tender but still firm.

2 Pour in the vegetable stock and add the beef tomatoes. Add the chickpeas, red lentils, red kidney beans, green green beans, and sunflower seeds. Stir in the tomato purée and add a splash each of Tabasco and soy sauce to taste.

3 Cook on the stove for 15 minutes over a medium heat until all the vegetables are cooked but still firm. Pour this mixture into the base of an ovenproof casserole dish. Season to taste and add the roughly chopped sage leaves.

4 To make the topping, boil the potatoes until soft. Mash them with low-fat sour cream and roughly crumble the Feta cheese into the mixture, reserving some for the top. Spread this mash over the vegetable mix and crumble the reserved Feta cheese on top.

5 Heat through in a preheated oven (325°F/170°C/Gas 3) until the top has browned. Serve like a country cottage pie with French beans or cabbage.

This dish is also delicious cold, sliced into lunchbox-size portions.

FAT: 6G (9%) • PROTEIN: 38G (76%) • CARBOHYDRATE: 109G (36%) • FIBER: 37G (147%)
VITAMIN A: 120% • FOLATE: 105% • IRON: 70% • CHOLESTEROL: 0

Riot of Chunky Vegetables

As well as a blast of the most potent antioxidant nutrients, this meal provides almost 50 percent of the minimum daily intake of vitamin D. Crucial for bone growth, vitamin D helps the body use both calcium and phosphorous. We cannot utilize the vitamin D we get directly from either our diet or supplements, but must convert it first to an active form. This job is carried out by the liver, which is why people with liver and kidney disease are at a higher risk of osteoporosis (brittle bone disease) than others.

SERVES 6

1 head of cauliflower, cut into florets	**3¼ cups (800ml) soy milk**
6 large carrots, cut into chunks	**1 egg yolk**
1 medium rutabaga, cut into chunks	**½ cup (125g) Emmental cheese, grated**
5 large potatoes, cut into chunks	**3 tbsp chopped fresh flat-leaf parsley**
3 fresh sage leaves	**1 pinch of freshly grated nutmeg**
4 tbsp soy spread	**freshly ground black pepper**
4 tbsp white flour	**6 hardboiled eggs, shelled**

1 Cook the cauliflower, carrots, rutabaga, and potatoes with the sage leaves in boiling water until tender but still firm. Drain and rinse.

2 Melt the soy spread in a heavy-based pan. Add the flour and whisk well. Cook for 2–3 minutes, then start adding the cold milk, a little at a time, stirring constantly.

3 Bring to a gentle boil and cook for another 2 minutes. Add the egg yolk, Emmental (reserving a little to top the dish), chopped parsley, and grated nutmeg. Season.

4 Put all the cooked vegetables in an ovenproof dish. Cut the hard-boiled eggs in half and arrange in the same dish. Pour over the white cheese sauce and sprinkle the reserved cheese over the top. Bake in a preheated oven (350°F/180°C/Gas 4) for 20–25 minutes until the top is golden brown. Serve with garlic and rosemary bread *(see page 38)* and a side salad of mixed green leaves.

If you like, try adding 3½oz (100g) of tuna to the white sauce before baking.

Fat: 20g (31%) • Protein: 23g (46%) • Carbohydrate: 47g (16%)
Fiber: 7g (28%) • Vitamin A: 440% • Vitamin C: 160% • Vitamin D: 47%
Potassium: 160% • Cholesterol: 89%

Spicy French Beans with Pine Nuts

In general, the darker and more intensely colored the vegetable, the higher its levels of nutrients. This high-fiber, zero-cholesterol side dish contains bright-green parsley, which is an excellent source of vitamins. In fact, parsley is so potent that you only need to eat very small amounts. Parsley helps support adrenal and thyroid functions, aids digestion, and contains a chemical said to prevent the multiplication of tumor cells. It is also used traditionally as a breath freshener.

SERVES 4

6 cups (800g) French beans	**4 tbsp pine kernels, roasted**
4 tbsp olive oil	**2 garlic cloves, crushed**
2 shallots, diced	**6 tbsp chopped fresh flat-leaf parsley**
1 red chili, deseeded and chopped	**freshly ground black pepper**

1 Cook the French beans until *al dente* (cooked but slightly crunchy) in plenty of boiling water. To stop the cooking and fix the luxuriant green chlorophyll color, drop them in a pan of cold water as soon as they are cooked.

2 Heat the olive oil in a wok and sauté the diced shallots, chili, pine kernels, and garlic for 5 minutes. Add the French beans and parsley. Season, sauté for a few more minutes, and serve immediately.

Fat: 22g (33%) • Protein: 8g (16%) • Carbohydrate: 23g (8%)
Fiber: 9g (37%) • Vitamin C: 100% • Potassium: 70% • Cholesterol: 0

Glazed Yams

Potent anticancer agents, yams are so effective that one study by The National Cancer Institute in the United States found that men who ate half a cup of yams every day were half as likely to develop lung cancer as those who ate almost none. Yams are included in the list of sources of phytochemicals that a growing number of researchers now believe can not only prevent many degenerative diseases but actually reverse them.

SERVES 4

6 yams (in total 1lb 12oz (800g)	**1in (2.5cm) fresh root ginger, grated**
4 tbsp brown sugar	**1 pinch of freshly grated nutmeg**
4 tbsp honey	
5 tsp orange juice	**freshly ground black pepper**

1 Boil the yams in plenty of water until just tender. Drain and cut into slices 1in (2.5cm) in length. Arrange these in a flat, ovenproof dish.

2 Combine the sugar, honey, orange juice, grated ginger, and nutmeg in a bowl. Pour this mixture over the yams. Season and cook in a preheated oven (400°F/200°C/Gas 6) until golden.

As an alternative to yams, try using parsnips or rutabagas.

FAT: 0.5G (1%) • PROTEIN: 3G (6%) • CARBOHYDRATE: 77G (26%)
FIBER: 4G (15%) • VITAMIN A: 680% • VITAMIN C: 60% • CHOLESTEROL: 0

Ladies' Fingers (Okra) with Lime

Okra can help protect the intestinal tract. It can relieve irritation of the lining of the gut and is effective against disorders such as stomach ulcers and colitis. The folate in this dish can help improve skin condition and its cholesterol-lowering, antioxidant vitamin C will help fight cancer.

SERVES 6

5 cups (1kg) ladies' fingers (okra)	**3 tsp ground cumin**
3 scallions, sliced	**freshly ground black pepper**
3 garlic cloves, crushed	**juice of 2 limes**
4 tbsp olive oil	**2 sprigs of fresh flat-leaf parsley**
1 red pepper, diced	

1 Trim the okra and slice into ½in (1cm) pieces.
2 Cook the scallions and garlic in olive oil for 5 minutes. Add the okra, red pepper, and cumin. Season and cook for 15 minutes until the okra is soft. Just before serving, add the lime juice and chopped parsley.

To make this into a main course dish, add shrimp.

FAT: 10G (15%) • PROTEIN: 5G (8%) • CARBOHYDRATE: 15G (5%)
FIBER: 5G (19%) • VITAMIN C: 90% • FOLATE: 20% • CHOLESTEROL: 0

Tian of Summer Vegetables

This is a traditional dish from the South of France where rates of heart disease are low, despite a high-fat diet washed down with lots of red wine. The eggplants prevent the rise of blood cholesterol, protect the arteries from plaque deposits, and enhance the immune system. The high potassium content, which regulates heartbeat, will also help to keep your muscles and your nervous system healthy.

SERVES 6

2 garlic cloves, crushed

3 onions, chopped

¾ cup (175ml) olive oil

1 tsp coriander seeds

6 zucchini, cut into ¼in (½cm) slices

4 long, narrow eggplants, cut into ¼in (½cm) slices

6 medium tomatoes, cut into ¼in (½cm) slices

6 bay leaves

1 sprig of fresh thyme

1 sprig of fresh oregano

3 star anise, crushed

1 Sauté the crushed garlic and chopped onion in 3 tablespoonfuls of the olive oil for 5 minutes, until slightly golden. Mix in the coriander seeds. In a large, flat, ovenproof dish, spread out the onion and coriander seed mix so that it covers the entire tray.

2 On top of this, arrange the sliced vegetables neatly in alternate rows starting with the zucchini in one line, the eggplants in the next, followed by the tomatoes. Continue this sequence until the entire tray has been covered with the sliced vegetables.

3 Slide the bay leaves between these rows. Strip the oregano and thyme leaves from their stems and sprinkle the leaves on top of the rows of vegetables, together with the crushed star anise.

4 Pour the remaining olive oil evenly over the top of all the herbs and vegetables. Cook slowly in a preheated oven (225°F/110°C/Gas ¼) for 1½ hours. You can serve this dish hot or cold.

Avoid eggplants if you suffer from arthritis.

FAT: 29G (44%) • PROTEIN: 5G (10%) • CARBOHYDRATE: 37G (12%)
FIBER: 12G (49%) • VITAMIN C: 70% • POTASSIUM: 152% • CHOLESTEROL: 0

Roasted Celeriac with Sage

Lack of vitamin B_2 (riboflavin) is one of the most common nutritional deficiencies among adults in the United States. To improve your levels of riboflavin, try this recipe, full of vitamin B-rich celeriac. Unlike its close relative vitamin B_1 (thiamine), riboflavin is not destroyed by heat. Also known as vitamin G, riboflavin boosts the immune system, helps regulate hormones, improves skin condition, and helps relieve stress. Oats, another ingredient, also keep you calm, making this a superb stress-busting dish. In addition, oats are one of the most effective cholesterol-lowering foods and are an excellent aid for the digestion.

SERVES 6

5 cups (1kg) celeriac, peeled

1 sprig of fresh thyme

5 garlic cloves, left in the skin

½ cup (125ml) olive oil

freshly ground black pepper

1 cup (150g) rolled oats

15 fresh sage leaves, chopped

1 Dice the celeriac into 1¼in (3cm) square cubes and blanch them in boiling water. Drain and dry them with paper towels. Lay out the celeriac cubes with the thyme and garlic cloves in a deep roasting tray.

2 Pour over the olive oil, season, and cook in a preheated oven (400°F/200°C/Gas 6) for 20 minutes.

3 Sprinkle the oats into the dish and cook for another 10 minutes until the celeriac is golden colored and crispy. Just before serving, top with the chopped sage leaves.

FAT: 19G (29%) • PROTEIN: 6G (12%) • CARBOHYDRATE: 30G (10%)
FIBER: 5G (20%) • VITAMIN B_2: 10% • VITAMIN C: 20% • CHOLESTEROL: 0

Swiss Chard— Two Ways

This power-packed, anticancer dish could not be simpler or healthier. Chard corrects calcium deficiency, regulates digestive function, and acts as a diuretic. The chlorophyll-rich leaves will also help keep your breath fresh.

SERVES 6

For the first way:	For the second way:
32 cups (1.5kg) Swiss chard	**32 cups (1.5kg) Swiss chard**
⅛ cup (100g) fresh Parmesan cheese, grated	**2 garlic cloves, crushed**
½ cup (50g) breadcrumbs	**1 sprig each of fresh rosemary and thyme**
freshly ground black pepper	**4 tbsp olive oil**
4 tbsp vegetable stock	**freshly ground black pepper**
	½ cup (50g) fresh flat-leaf parsley, chopped

For the first way:

1 Wash and dry the Swiss chard and separate the green leaves from the white ribs, reserving both. Blanch the leaves in boiling water, drain, and dry. Mix the Parmesan with the breadcrumbs and season.

2 In a flat-bottomed, ovenproof dish, start to build layers of chard and cheese, like a lasagne. Start with the chard leaves and ribs and finish with the Parmesan. To keep the dish moist, pour the vegetable stock over each of these layers.

3 Bake for 25 minutes in an oven preheated to 350°F/180°C/Gas 4 until the cheese has browned.

For the second way:

1 Separate the chard leaves from the ribs as before. Cut the ribs into small strips and, in a casserole dish on the stove, cook them and the green leaves along with the crushed garlic, rosemary, and thyme in olive oil until tender but still firm.

2 Season, cover, and cook for 20 minutes over a medium heat. Add the parsley and stir well before serving.

> FAT: 16G (24%) • PROTEIN: 13G (26%) • CARBOHYDRATE: 17G (6%)
> FIBER: 5G (19%) • VITAMIN A: 180% • VITAMIN C: 140% • CALCIUM: 17MG (47%)
> POTASSIUM: 118% • CHOLESTEROL: 4%

Braised Fennel

A natural appetite suppressant, fennel is a useful food for weight-loss management. It can also relieve the symptoms of irritable bowel syndrome (IBS) and works to support the liver, kidneys, and spleen. High in the antioxidant vitamins A and C, it has anticancer properties, strengthens the immune system, and can help to keep the lungs clear.

SERVES 6

4 large fennel bulbs	**2 bay leaves**
½ lemon (not consumed)	**1 sprig of fresh thyme**
1 onion, sliced	**freshly ground black pepper**
2 carrots, sliced	**½ cup (50g) fresh parsley, chopped, to garnish**
3 cups (750ml) vegetable (or chicken) stock	

1 Trim, wash, and remove both the stalks and the leaves from the fennel bulbs. Cook in boiling water with the lemon half for 15 minutes. Discard the lemon. Drain well and cut the fennel in half, lengthwise.

2 Put the sliced onion and carrots in the bottom of a casserole dish. Add the fennel, cover with the stock, and add the bay leaves and thyme. Season.

3 Cover with a tight-fitting lid. If you don't have one, cover the dish with waxed paper. Cook in a preheated oven (275°F/140°C/Gas 1) for 1½ hours. Serve garnished with chopped fresh parsley.

You can braise any type of vegetable in this way.

> FAT: 1G (1%) • PROTEIN: 3G (6%) • CARBOHYDRATE: 18G (6%)
> FIBER: 6G (25%) • VITAMIN A: 110% • VITAMIN C: 60% • CHOLESTEROL: 0

DESSERTS

Banana and Rosemary Tatin

Everyone knows bananas are rich in energy-giving potassium, which protects the heart, but it's less well known that they feed the "good" bacteria in the digestive tract, improving the digestion. Bananas encourage the production of serotonin, a mood-enhancing hormone, and, because they are low in fat, they are a useful weight-control aid. Rosemary stimulates the circulation, maintains healthy blood pressure, and is an antibacterial agent. It can relieve migraines and, in folklore, it is said to improve concentration and memory.

SERVES 6

12 bananas	1 sprig of fresh rosemary
juice of 1 lemon	4 tbsp roasted almond flakes
2 tbsp soy spread	10½oz (300g) puff pastry
½ cup (125g) superfine sugar	½ cup (125ml) water

1 Cut the bananas into 2⅓in (6cm) batons and mix them with the lemon juice. Line the bottom of a round, shallow (7in/18cm diameter) tart tin or flan dish with waxed paper. The tin should have an attached, nonremovable bottom.

2 Melt the soy spread and sugar in a pan. Bring to a gentle boil, cook until the liquid turns a golden caramel color, then pour it into the tart tin.

3 Place a few leaves of fresh rosemary in the sauce and arrange the banana batons, standing upright, in a very tight circle to cover the entire bottom of the tin. Insert the roasted almond flakes between the banana batons.

4 Roll the puff pastry out to form a circle that is ⅛in (3mm) thick and at least 1¼in (3cm) wider in circumference than the tart tin. Cover the bananas and fold the excess pastry down in between the edge of the tin and the outside ring of banana. (The puff pastry will eventually become the base of the tatin when it is turned upside down.)

5 Make a hole in the middle of the secured pastry to release steam and pour in the water to create a sauce and stop the caramel from burning while the fruit cooks. Place in a preheated oven (375°F/190°C/Gas 5) for 20–25 minutes until the puff pastry is cooked. When you take the tin out of the oven, place a large plate or tray over the top and, carefully but quickly, turn the tin and the tray upside down.

6 Leave the tatin to rest for 15 minutes, then gently remove the tin. Do not force it. If it sticks, use a sharp-edged knife to free the pastry edges from the dish. Serve warm on its own or with vanilla ice cream. *(See also page 116 for Pineapple and Papaya Ice Cream recipe.)*

Tatin means "reversed" so you make this dish, cook it, and turn it upside down to present it.

FAT: 24G (37%) • PROTEIN: 7G (14%) • CARBOHYDRATE: 104G (35%) • FIBER: 7G (27%)
VITAMIN C: 40% • POTASSIUM: 110% • CHOLESTEROL: 10%

Strawberry Soup with Red Wine

A powerful antioxidant, strawberries can protect against DNA damage and ounce for ounce contain more fiber than whole-wheat bread. High in potassium, strawberries also act as antiviral agents and are effective against the herpes virus, which causes cold sores. Red wine is believed to contain a nonalcoholic chemical that may prevent the formation of the plaque that blocks the arteries increasing the risk of stroke and heart disease. The fresh mint in this dish will lessen the length of time food spends in the stomach by stimulating gastric juices and can also help relieve insomnia and migraines.

SERVES 6   ② ③ ❹ ❽

1 cup (250g) superfine sugar

3½ cups (900ml) red wine

2 standard tea bags

10 green peppercorns

8 cups (1.2kg) fresh strawberries

20 fresh mint leaves, chopped

1 Bring the sugar, wine, tea bags, and green peppercorns to a boil in a pan and cook until the liquid thickens. Strain and return to the pan.

2 Wash the strawberries and drain them well. Take the tails off and cut each one in two. Add them to the liquid in the pan and cook for 3 minutes. Serve in small bowls, sprinkled with chopped mint leaves.

In France, this dish is served either warm or ice cold.

> FAT: 1G (1%) (SATURATED FAT: 0) • PROTEIN: 2G (4%) • CARBOHYDRATE: 59G (20%)
> FIBER: 5G (18%) • VITAMIN C: 200% • POTASSIUM: 56% • CHOLESTEROL: 0

Pain d'Epices

The Japanese serve ginger slices between sushi courses to cleanse the palate and aid digestion. In the West, ginger has long been used to settle the stomach, but it can also relieve stiff muscles and aching joints. The star anise in this rustic and old-fashioned dish also promotes healthy digestion and increases mental clarity. You'll be hard pressed to find another dessert that is as low in fat—it has less than a gram of saturated fats—and as rich in dietary fiber as this delicious bread-type pudding.

SERVES 8   ② ③ ❹ ⑥

½ cup (125ml) organic milk (use soy if intolerant to lactose)

1 tsp ground ginger

1 cinnamon stick

8 cloves

2 tsp star anise

½ cup (100g) sugar

1½ cups (325ml) maple syrup, plus ½ cup to glaze

1⅔ cups (250g) white flour (use gluten-free if intolerant)

1⅔ cups (250g) rye flour

2 tsp baking powder (gluten-free if intolerant)

3 eggs, beaten

1 Bring the milk to a boil, add the spices, and let it infuse for 30 minutes. Strain the milk, add the sugar and maple syrup, and rewarm the mixture.

2 In a bowl, combine the two flours and the baking powder. Slowly add the warm milk and the eggs and mix well. Line a 1lb (500g) loaf tin with greaseproof paper and pour in the loaf mix.

3 Bake in a preheated oven (350°F/180°C/Gas 4) for 1 hour. To check if the loaf is cooked, pierce the center with a thin metal skewer and pull back out. If it comes out dry, it is done. Remove from the tin and brush the whole loaf with maple syrup.

This dish always tastes better 24 hours after cooking, when all the flavors have fully infused the loaf. Slice and serve with Quick Confiture *(see page 114)* or pack for a picnic lunch.

> FAT: 3.5G (6%) • PROTEIN: 9G (18%) • CARBOHYDRATE: 106G (35%)
> FIBER: 6G (25%) • VITAMIN B3: 23% • IRON: 20% • POTASSIUM: 55%
> CHOLESTEROL: 27%

Summer Honey and Lavender Crème Brulée

Even the name of this dish conjures up an uplifting picture of the perfect English summer with the bees buzzing around the lavender flowers. The bees' honey and the plants' flowers combine in this Catalan-inspired dish. The healing power of honey, nature's sweetener, is well documented. It can help treat an enormous number of disorders, from acne to rheumatism. Lavender has an antidepressant, calming effect and helps lower blood pressure. Eat this dessert as a special treat when you need cheering up.

SERVES 6 ❸❹❻❼

4 egg yolks	**2½ cups (600ml) soy cream**
2 tbsp cornstarch	**2 tbsp honey**
⅔ cup (150g) superfine sugar	**6 lavender flowerheads**

1 Whisk the egg yolks, cornstarch, and ½ cup (100g) of the sugar together until the mixture is white and foamy.

2 In a pan, gently heat the soy cream, honey, and lavender flowers until just below boiling point. (You will see the surface just begin to bubble.) Pass the hot liquid through a fine sieve into the bowl containing the foamy egg and sugar mixture, whisking constantly.

3 Return the mixture to the pan and cook very slowly until the custard thickens. Remove from the heat and keep stirring until it has cooled and is just warm.

4 Pour the custard into six small ramekin dishes and chill until cold. Before serving, cover the top of each dish with the reserved sugar. Pop under a hot broiler to caramelize the top. It should be crispy and golden brown.

FAT: 34G (52%) • PROTEIN: 6G (12%) • CARBOHYDRATE: 96G (32%)
VITAMIN D: 8% • PHOSPHOROUS: 47% • POTASSIUM: 84% • CHOLESTEROL: 48%

Honey and Fig Loaf

High in fiber, figs fight cancer, can ward off bacterial infections, and may be eaten as a natural laxative. They can also help prevent painful hemorrhoids and are often fed to convalescing patients because they can speed up recovery from illness. Pure honey contains 180 different nutrients and curative substances; it is also the best form of carbohydrate for human consumption because it is the most easily digested.

SERVES 6 ❷❹❻❽

1¼ cups (175g) whole-wheat flour (use gluten-free if intolerant)	**⅔ cup (150ml) organic milk (use soy milk if lactose-intolerant)**
½ tsp salt	**½ tsp bicarbonate of soda**
2 tbsp honey	**½ cup (100g) dried figs**

1 Mix the flour and salt in a large bowl and form a well in the center. Melt the honey in half the milk on the stove and dissolve the bicarbonate of soda in the reserved cold milk.

2 Take the warmed milk and honey off the stove and combine it with the cold milk and bicarbonate of soda. Pour the milk into the well in the middle of the flour. Add the dried figs and mix well.

3 Transfer this mixture to a 1lb (500g) loaf tin, which you have lined with waxed paper. Cook in a preheated oven (325°F/170°C/Gas 3) for about 40 minutes until you can pierce the loaf with a skewer and it comes out clean. Let the loaf rest for a few hours before eating.

You can replace the figs with dried apricots or sultanas.

FAT: 1G (1%) • PROTEIN: 5G (10%) • CARBOHYDRATE: 39G (13%)
FIBER: 6G (22%) • IRON: 8% • POTASSIUM: 31% • CHOLESTEROL: 0

Quick Confiture— Guava or Pineapple

Change the fruit and see how the nutritional breakdown of the entire dish changes. Guava is high in fiber and crammed with stress-busting, cancer-fighting vitamin C. Pineapple has relatively little vitamin C but the lemon juice compensates for this. Pineapple contains an enzyme called bromelain, which has powerful anti-inflammatory and digestive properties. It enhances the absorption of other nutrients and is now believed to be beneficial to the cardiovascular system as well.

SERVES 4

For Guava Confiture:	1¾ cups (400ml) water
4 cups (500g) guava	**¼ vanilla pod**
1¼ cups (250g) sugar	**juice of 1 lemon**

1 Wash and remove the head of the guava. Peel and cut the fruit into slices and discard the excess seeds.
2 In a heavy-based pan, dissolve the sugar in the water; add the fruit, vanilla, and lemon juice. Cook slowly for 1 hour, until the fruit is very soft. Serve warm or cold the same day.

For Pineapple Confiture:	**¼ vanilla pod**
1 large fresh pineapple	**juice of 1 lemon**
1 cup (200g) sugar	
⅞ cup (200ml) water	

1 Peel the pineapple and dice into small cubes.
2 Dissolve the sugar in the water, add the pineapple, vanilla pod, and lemon juice. Cook for 30–45 minutes, until the fruit is soft.

GUAVA: FAT: 1G (2%) • PROTEIN: 1G (2%) • CARBOHYDRATE: 78G (26%)
FIBER: 7G (27%) • VITAMIN A: 20% • VITAMIN C: 390% • CHOLESTEROL: 0
PINEAPPLE: FAT: 0.5G (1%) • PROTEIN: 1G (2%) • CARBOHYDRATE: 79G (26%)
FIBER: 2G (6%) • VITAMIN C: 35% • MANGANESE: 8% • CHOLESTEROL: 0

Carrot and Walnut Cake

Energizing carrots, which detoxify and cleanse the body, contain large quantities of betacarotenes, which are potent anticancer agents. Carrots can slow the growth of "bad" bacteria in the digestive tract and will improve the quality of hair, skin, and nails. They can counter stress, protect against macular degeneration (eye disease), and if eaten every day, help regulate the menstrual cycle. Walnuts are high in vitamin A, potassium, magnesium, and omega-3 fatty acids.

SERVES 6

1 cup (200g) sugar	**2 tsp baking powder**
1 tbsp walnut oil	**1 large carrot, grated**
5 tsp vanilla extract	**⅓ cup (50g) sultanas**
4 eggs, beaten	**½ cup (80g) walnuts, chopped**
1¾ cups (250g) whole-wheat flour (use gluten-free, if intolerant)	

1 Mix together the sugar, oil, and vanilla extract. Add the eggs, one by one, stirring vigorously. Add the flour, baking powder, grated carrots, sultanas, and walnuts.
2 Transfer this mixture to a 1lb (500g) loaf tin lined with waxed paper. Cook for 1 hour in a preheated oven (325°F/160°C/Gas 3). Pierce the center with a metal skewer. If it comes out clean, the cake is done.

Leave this cake to rest for 3–4 hours so that it is stone cold before you cut it.

FAT: 22G (34%) • PROTEIN: 13G (26%) • CARBOHYDRATE: 44G (15%)
FIBER: 7G (28%) • VITAMIN A: 100% • IRON: 15% • POTASSIUM: 100%
CHOLESTEROL: 47%

Pineapple and Papaya Ice Cream

Papaya can be given to help babies on infant formula digest their milk. It soothes digestive disorders and helps break down unwanted toxins, including uric acid, in the body. Soy (or bean curd) contains probably the most powerful of the phytochemicals, which is said to reverse many diseases, including cancer, heart disease, and diabetes. Aim to eat at least one serving of soy protein a day, but make sure the product you use has not been genetically modified. This nondairy ice cream is suitable for the lactose-intolerant.

SERVES 6

1 cup (200g) fresh pineapple, peeled and cored

½ cup (100g) fresh papaya, peeled and deseeded

1 cup (200g) sugar

⅞ cup (200ml) soy cream

For the vanilla custard:

6 tbsp superfine sugar

6 egg yolks

2 cups (500ml) soy milk

2 vanilla pods, split in half, lengthwise

1 To make the custard, whisk the sugar and the egg yolks in a large bowl until pale and foaming. In a pan, bring the milk and vanilla pods to boiling point. Take off the heat, strain, and pour the infused milk gently onto the egg mixture, whisking constantly.

2 Transfer this mixture back to the pan and cook very gently, over a medium heat, stirring with a metal spoon until the liquid coats the back of the spoon. Take off the heat and transfer to a bowl to cool.

3 Purée the two fruits in a food processor. Transfer to a pan with the superfine sugar and cook gently for 20 minutes. Leave to cool.

4 When both mixtures are completely cold, combine them with the soy cream and transfer everything to a deep-freezer container. Leave the ice cream mixture to set in the freezer, taking it out and whisking it every 20 minutes or so, until it has hardened. Serve the ice cream with fresh pineapple and papaya slices.

FAT: 10G (16%) • PROTEIN: 6G (12%) • CARBOHYDRATE: 56G (19%)
FIBER: 2G (7%) • VITAMIN C: 25% • IRON: 8% • POTASSIUM: 32% • CHOLESTEROL: 71%

Passion Fruit Salad

We all know we should eat lots of fresh fruit if we want to be healthy, but lots of people make the mistake of eating fruit straight after a meal. Fruit will actually make certain digestive disorders worse if you eat it with other food. Instead, eat fruit or this fruit salad for breakfast, as a snack, or as a dessert, but wait half an hour after your main course. Most people think of oranges when they crave vitamin C but, in fact, Kiwifruit are a richer source of this important antioxidant and also provide vitamin K, which can help repair thread and varicose veins.

SERVES 6

1 cup (250ml) fresh orange juice

1 cup (250ml) water

1 cup (200g) brown sugar

½ pineapple, peeled and diced

3 Kiwifruit, peeled and diced

3 mandarin oranges, broken into segments

2 mangoes, peeled and diced

15 fresh mint leaves, chopped, plus extra to garnish

½ cup (50g) raspberries

½ cup (50g) red currants

5 passion fruit

2 bananas, optional

1 Bring the orange juice, water, and sugar to a boil in a pan. Remove from the heat and leave to cool.

2 Mix all the fruits except the raspberries, redcurrants, passion fruit, and bananas (if using) with the chopped mint leaves, and leave to chill for at least 6 hours in the refrigerator. Cover the dish to stop the fruit from drying out in the cold.

3 When ready to serve, mix the chilled fruits, the raspberries, and the redcurrants with the cold syrup. Cut the passion fruit in half, scoop out the pulp and mix with the fruit salad. Serve this dish very cold, garnished with chopped mint leaves.

For variety, experiment with the fruits you use. Be as adventurous as you like, but to prevent bananas discoloring, always mix them in at the end (if using), along with the red fruits (which otherwise will color the other fruits).

FAT: 1G (1%) • PROTEIN: 2G (4%) • CARBOHYDRATE: 68G (23%) • FIBER: 5G (20%)
VITAMIN A: 70% • VITAMIN C: 170% • VITAMIN K: 100% • CHOLESTEROL: 0

Rhubarb and Plum Flan

Another cholesterol-free dessert that, as well as helping to protect your heart, can aid digestion, relieve constipation, and support the liver. Rhubarb, which also has anticancer properties, has been shown to stimulate uterine contractions and has been used to regulate menstruation. Plums are a natural laxative; antiviral and antibacterial, they also help strengthen the immune system and keep infections at bay.

SERVES 6

4 cups (800g) rhubarb

1 cup (200g) plums, stoned and halved

1¼ cups (250g) brown sugar

4 tbsp water

10½oz (300g) puff pastry

½ cup (100g) apricot jam

2 tbsp rum

1 Wash, drain, and strip the stringy edges from the rhubarb stalks. Cut each one into 1in (2cm) lengths. Place the rhubarb, plums, brown sugar, and water in an ovenproof dish, cover with foil and cook for 15 minutes in a preheated oven (425°F/220°C/Gas 7). Let it cool.

2 Roll the puff pastry as thinly as possible and shape into a round. Use to line a 10in (25cm) flan dish. Prick with a fork.

3 Cover the base with the rhubarb and plum mixture and bake for 25 minutes in a preheated oven (400°F/200°C/Gas 6). When the flan is cooked, melt the apricot jam with the rum and pour over the top of the flan to glaze it.

For a special occasion, pour cold custard over the pastry base of the flan before piling on the fruit and cooking. (This will make the flan higher in fat.) You can also cook the rhubarb with other fruits; try apricot or peach.

FAT: 20G (30%) • PROTEIN: 5G (10%) • CARBOHYDRATE: 85G (28%) • FIBER: 4G (15%)
VITAMIN C: 25% • POTASSIUM: 70% • CHOLESTEROL: 10%

The**A-Team**

SERVES 4

CIABATTA BREAD WITH ROASTED VEGETABLES AND MOZZARELLA, VEGETABLE CHIPS, AND A CRUNCHY CRANBERRY BAR

Packed with almost six times the minimum daily requirement of immune-boosting, cancer-fighting vitamin A, and almost three times the minimum amount of vitamin C you need to keep disease at bay, this picnic will help fight cancers, increase immunity, banish stress, and give you more energy.

The Sandwich

1 onion, quartered	1 sprig of fresh oregano
2 large carrots, cut into chunks	4 cherry tomatoes
1 red pepper, deseeded and quartered	3 sprigs of fresh thyme
1 green pepper, quartered	freshly ground black pepper
2 small zucchini, cut into chunks	2 tbsp balsamic vinegar
6 garlic cloves, skins left on	4 mini ciabatta breads
½ cup (125ml) olive oil	½ cup (100g) mozzarella, sliced
	8 fresh basil leaves

1 In a large bowl, mix the vegetables with the garlic, olive oil, oregano, tomatoes, and thyme. Season. Pile all this onto a baking tray and cook in a preheated oven (425°F/220°C/Gas 7) for 25 minutes.
2 Remove from the oven, add the vinegar, and leave to cool. Now cut all the vegetables small enough to be eaten in a sandwich. Cut each ciabatta bread in half. Fill with the sliced mozzarella, chilled roasted vegetables, and fresh basil leaves.

FAT: 30G (46%) • PROTEIN: 15G (30%) • CARBOHYDRATE: 50G (17%)
FIBER: 7G (27%) • VITAMIN A: 450% • VITAMIN C: 170% • CALCIUM: 30%
CHOLESTEROL: 5%

The Chips

2 zucchini	2 raw beets, peeled
3 carrots, peeled	freshly ground black pepper
3 parsnips, peeled	
3 potatoes, peeled	

1 Slice the zucchini lengthwise into long, thin strips. Use a vegetable peeler to shave all the vegetables into slivers, trying to make the slivers as wide as you can because they will curl.
2 Place all the shavings on a baking tray which you have lined with waxed paper and dry-roast them in the oven on its lowest setting until they look like potato chips (about 15 minutes). Season to taste.

FAT: 0.5G (1%) • PROTEIN: 5G (10%) • CARBOHYDRATE: 41G (14%)
FIBER: 8G (34%) • VITAMIN A: 210% • VITAMIN C: 70% • POTASSIUM: 140%
CHOLESTEROL: 0

Cranberry Bar

⅔ cup (125g) raw brown sugar	1 cup (125g) soy flour
1 tbsp corn syrup	1 cup (125g) oat flakes
½ cup (125g) olive oil spread	½ cup (50g) dried cranberries

1 Put the sugar, corn syrup, and olive oil spread in a pan and melt gently over a low heat. When melted, add all the other ingredients and mix well.
2 Cover a baking pan with waxed paper and pour the mixture in. Cook in an oven preheated to (350°F/180°C/Gas 4) for 15–20 minutes. Leave to cool and slice into ten picnic bars.

You can replace the cranberries with any other kind of dried fruits, for example figs or prunes.

FAT: 9G (14%) • PROTEIN: 7G (14%) • CARBOHYDRATE: 26G (9%)
FIBER: 3G (13%) • VITAMIN A: 8% • VITAMIN E: 10% • IRON: 10%
CHOLESTEROL: 0

The**B-Team**

SERVES 4

PUMPKIN BREAD WITH AVOCADO, WATERCRESS, AND WALNUTS, CARROT AND PECAN SALAD, AND CHARENTAIS MELON BALLS

This power-packed picnic is full of the all-important B vitamins, without which not much happens in the body. B vitamins help maintain healthy skin, nerves, digestion, reproductive system, blood, circulation, and brainpower. Pumpkin seeds are rich in prostate-protecting zinc, bone-building calcium, and B vitamins.

The Salad

6 carrots, grated	½ cup (100g) mango, diced
juice of 1 lemon	½ cup (80g) sultanas
juice of 1 orange	6 tbsp olive oil
1 cup (100g) pecans, roasted	1 tbsp chopped fresh chives

1 Mix all the ingredients except the chives together and chill for at least 2 hours before you want to pack it. Sprinkle with chopped chives and eat.

FAT: 35G (54%) • PROTEIN: 4G (8%) • CARBOHYDRATE: 38G (13%)
FIBER: 7G (30%) • VITAMIN A: 580% • POTASSIUM: 71% • CHOLESTEROL: 0

Melon Balls

1 large Charentais melon	10 fresh mint leaves

1 Cut and deseed the melon. Use a melon baller to scoop the flesh out and mix with the chopped mint. If possible, chill before eating.

FAT: 0G (0%) • PROTEIN: 1G (2%) • CARBOHYDRATE: 14G (5%) • FIBER: LESS THAN 1G (4%) • VITAMIN C: 60% • POTASSIUM: 45% • CHOLESTEROL: 0

The Sandwich

	For the filling:
8oz (225g) pumpkin, diced	
1 tsp sugar	2 ripe avocados, sliced
5 tsp warm soy milk, plus extra to glaze	juice of 1 lemon
1 envelope dry yeast	1 bunch of watercress, roughly chopped
1¾ cups (225g) whole-wheat flour (use gluten-free if intolerant)	½ cup (50g) walnuts
½ tsp cinnamon	2 tsp pumpkin seeds, roasted
½ tsp ground ginger	4 tsp olive oil
1 pinch of freshly grated nutmeg	freshly ground black pepper
2 tbsp olive oil spread	4 tbsp olive oil spread
2 tsp salt	
2 tsp pumpkin seeds	

1 To make the pumpkin bread, cook the pumpkin in boiling water until tender. Drain and purée. Combine the sugar, milk, and yeast together in a bowl. Leave to stand for 10 minutes.

2 In another large bowl, mix the flour, spices, olive oil spread, and salt. Create a well in the middle and pour the yeast mixture and the puréed pumpkin into it. Use a knife to mix all the ingredients together lightly and then transfer to a well-floured surface.

3 Begin to knead the dough, adding more flour if it is too wet. Knead for at least 5 minutes and, when the dough is smooth, return to the bowl and leave it to double in size. Return it to your floured worktop, knead for 2–3 minutes then shape into a ball. Place on a baking sheet, cover, and leave to double in size in a warm place.

4 When ready, glaze the dough with milk and sprinkle pumpkin seeds on top. Bake in a preheated oven (400°F/200°C/Gas 6) for 30 minutes. When cooked, take the bread out of the oven, brush the top with milk and return to the oven for another 10 minutes until the top is shiny and crusty. Leave to cool.

5 To make the sandwich, arrange the avocados so they lie flat in a dish. Squeeze the lemon juice over the top to stop them from blackening. Add the watercress to the avocados along with the walnuts, pumpkin seeds, and olive oil.

6 Season to taste and leave to chill for 5 minutes. Slice the pumpkin bread, top with the olive oil spread and pile on the filling.

FAT: 53G (81%) • PROTEIN: 10G (20%) • CARBOHYDRATE: 73G (24%)
FIBER: 7G (30%) • VITAMIN B_3: 48% • VITAMIN B_6: 25% • CALCIUM: 6%
FOLATE: 21% • ZINC: 10% • CHOLESTEROL: 18%

The**San-Fran** Special

SERVES 4

SAN FRANCISCO BAGELS WITH CREAM CHEESE,
DILL, AND SMOKED SALMON,
MINI STUFFED VINE LEAVES, AND FRESH FIGS

The so-called oily fish, which include salmon,
are a good source of vitamins A and D and are rich in the
omega-3 fatty acids that help lower cholesterol and high
blood pressure. Researchers have also found a link between
increased rates of depression and a decline in the
consumption of oily fish. Omega-3s are fragile substances
that can be destroyed by heat, but in this picnic meal, the
salmon is smoked rather than cooked, so this is clearly
not a problem. Thanks to the figs, which are high in fiber,
this picnic also has an anticancer action.

②③④⑦⑧⑩

The Bagel

4 bagels	freshly ground black pepper
1 cup (250g) low-fat cream cheese	
2 tbsp chopped fresh dill	4 slices smoked salmon

1 Slice the bagels in two and toast to a golden brown.
Mix the cream cheese with the dill and season to taste.
2 Cut the salmon into ¼in (5mm) wide strips. Fill the
bagels with the cream cheese and smoked salmon.

FAT: 14G (22%) • PROTEIN: 24G (48%) • CARBOHYDRATE: 42G (14%)
FIBER: 2G (7%) • VITAMIN A: 10% • VITAMIN D: 80% • CALCIUM: 15% • FOLATE: 18%
IRON: 20% • CHOLESTEROL: 10%

The Stuffed Vine Leaves

1 large onion, diced	½ tsp ground turmeric
3 garlic cloves, crushed	freshly ground black pepper
4 tbsp olive oil	
1 large eggplant, peeled and diced	¼ cup (50g) Feta cheese, diced
4 tbsp sun-dried tomatoes, diced	10 pitted black olives, chopped
1 cup (200g) brown rice	½ cup (50g) fresh flat-leaf parsley, chopped
2 cups (500ml) vegetable stock	2 tbsp balsamic vinegar
	12 vine leaves (in brine)

1 Cook the onion and garlic in the olive oil for 10 minutes
until tender but not browned. Add the diced eggplant and
sun-dried tomatoes and cook for another 5 minutes. Add
the rice and stir to coat every grain.
2 Add the stock and the ground turmeric and season.
Cover and cook on a low heat for 20 minutes or until the
liquid has evaporated and the rice is tender. Add the Feta
cheese, olives, and chopped parsley and leave to cool.
3 When the rice is cold, mix in the vinegar and check the
seasoning. Lay the vine leaves out, one at a time, on a work
surface and place a tablespoonful of the filling at the
bottom of each leaf. Roll up the leaf tightly to create a mini
parcel. Do this with all 12 leaves and chill in the
refrigerator until you are ready to pack your picnic lunch.
Pack with the bagels and fresh figs.

FAT: 17G (27%) • PROTEIN: 9G (18%) • CARBOHYDRATE: 54G (18%)
FIBER: 5G (20%) • VITAMIN A: 25% • VITAMIN C: 30% • POTASSIUM: 71%
CHOLESTEROL: 4%

The Fresh Figs

8 fresh figs

FAT: 0 • PROTEIN: 1G (2%) • CARBOHYDRATE: 19G (6%) • FIBER: 3G (13%)
VITAMIN C: 4% • POTASSIUM: 26% • CHOLESTEROL: 0

InA**Nutshell**

SERVES 4

WHOLE-WHEAT PITTA WITH HOMEMADE HUMMUS
AND VEGETABLE SALAD, LIMA BEAN,
PASTA, AND BRAZIL NUT SALAD, AND BANANA
AND ALMOND WHEAT-FREE MUFFIN

With brazil nuts, sesame seed paste, chickpeas, almonds, and lima beans, this fiber-packed picnic will help protect against colon cancer, which is rapidly becoming the biggest killer in developed countries. It also combats digestive disorders such as irritable bowel syndrome, which is becoming a modern-day scourge: more working days are lost to IBS than to back pain, for example.

The Sandwich

1 large carrot, grated	**1 cup (200g) hummus** (*see below*)
¼ small red cabbage, grated	
1 small head lettuce, shredded	*For the hummus:*
½ cup (80g) celery, finely sliced	**2 cups (400g) chickpeas, soaked**
½ cup (80g) cucumber, finely sliced	**1 onion, diced**
2 tbsp chopped fresh flat-leaf parsley	**4 garlic cloves, crushed**
	4 tbsp tahini (sesame seed paste)
freshly ground black pepper	**juice of 3 lemons**
	1 pinch paprika
4 whole-wheat pitta breads	**1 tbsp chopped fresh parsley**

1 To make the hummus, cook the soaked chickpeas for 3–4 hours, skimming the surface scum off the water. When cooked, drain and transfer to a food processor. Add the onion, garlic, and tahini, and blend until smooth.
2 Finish with lemon juice and season to taste. Chill thoroughly and serve with paprika and chopped parsley sprinkled on top.
3 To make the pitta sandwich, mix all the vegetables with the parsley and season to taste. Toast the pitta breads, slice them open and spread a generous layer of homemade hummus inside. Pack each one full of the vegetable mix and wrap individually ready for the picnic.

FAT: 6G (9%) • PROTEIN: 10G (20%) • CARBOHYDRATE: 51G (17%)
FIBER: 9G (37%) • VITAMIN A: 150% • VITAMIN C: 45% • CHOLESTEROL: 0

The Salad

1½ cups (300g) lima beans, soaked	**½ cup (100g) brazil nuts, chopped**
1 pinch of turmeric	**5 tbsp chopped fresh cilantro**
1¾ cups (200g) whole-wheat pasta	**juice of 2 limes**
1 red pepper, diced	**4 tbsp olive oil**
1 onion, finely sliced	**freshly ground black pepper**

1 Cook the lima beans with the turmeric for at least 2 hours until tender and drain. Cook the pasta in boiling water and drain.
2 Mix the beans and pasta with the pepper, onion, brazil nuts, cilantro, lime juice, and olive oil, reserving a little cilantro to garnish. Season and serve very cold, garnished with chopped cilantro.

FAT: 29G (45%) • PROTEIN: 12G (24%) • CARBOHYDRATE: 35G (12%)
FIBER: 9G (35%) • VITAMIN C: 100% • IRON: 20% • CHOLESTEROL: 0

The Muffin

2 cups (300g) rice flour	**1 cup (250ml) soy milk**
1 tsp baking powder	**2 drops vanilla extract**
2 tbsp dark brown sugar	**½ cup (50g) semidried banana**
1 pinch of salt	
4 tbsp margarine	**4 tbsp almonds, chopped**
1 egg, beaten	

1 Mix the rice flour, baking powder, and sugar with a pinch of salt. Add the margarine, beaten egg, soy milk, and vanilla extract and stir until blended but not too smooth.
2 Dice the semidried bananas and add them to the batter with the chopped almonds. Pour this mixture into a muffin tin until it is two-thirds full. Cook for 25 minutes in a preheated oven (375°F/190°C/Gas 5).
3 When cooked, leave to cool and, when cold, pack in airtight containers ready for your picnic lunch.

FAT: 14G (21%) • PROTEIN: 7G (14%) • CARBOHYDRATE: 60G (20%)
FIBER: 4G (15%) • VITAMIN E: 25% • CALCIUM: 20% • POTASSIUM: 45%
CHOLESTEROL: 10%

Lunchbox**Spice**

SERVES 4

MIXED GRAIN BREAD WITH STIR-FRIED CHICKEN
AND WATER CHESTNUTS, SPICY AIOLI CROÛTONS,
AND BLACKBERRY SHORTCAKE

Turn back the clock with this antiaging, anticancer lunch
that contains high levels of selenium as well as plenty of
calcium and folate. Selenium is crucial for the manufacture
of glutathione peroxidase, the body's main antioxidant,
which is found in every single cell. In some trials, people
taking regular doses of selenium were half as likely to die
of cancer than those who did not take the mineral.
Researchers now believe selenium plays a purely
preventative role, stopping cancer from
developing in the first place.

The Sandwich

1½ cups (300g) chicken, cut into strips	1 scallion, chopped
4 tsp sesame oil (or olive oil)	4 tsp rice vinegar
¼ tsp Chinese five spice	6 cups (800g) water chestnuts, sliced
2 tbsp soy sauce	8 slices mixed grain bread
1 tbsp sesame seeds, toasted	

1 Sauté the chicken strips in the sesame oil for 2 minutes.
Add the Chinese five spice, soy sauce, and sesame seeds.
Cook for another 5–6 minutes, put to one side and let
it cool.

2 In a mixing bowl, combine the cooked chicken with the
scallion, rice vinegar, and the water chestnuts. Fill your
sandwiches with this delicious mixture and store in an
airtight container.

FAT: 10G (15%) • PROTEIN: 8G (16%) • CARBOHYDRATE: 36G (12%)
FIBER: 5G (21%) • IRON: 15% • SELENIUM: 41% • CHOLESTEROL: 0

The Croûtons

2 large potatoes, cut into chunks	1 cup (250ml) olive oil
6 garlic cloves	juice of 1 lemon
½ tsp turmeric	freshly ground black pepper
1 egg, beaten	1 French baguette

1 Boil the potato chunks in water until tender. Drain. Put
the garlic cloves in a pan of cold water, bring to a boil, and
drain. Repeat this procedure twice more to blanch the
cloves.

2 In a food processor, blend the potatoes, turmeric, egg, and
blanched garlic, and after 10 seconds drizzle in the olive
oil, little by little, as if making mayonnaise. Add the lemon
juice, check the seasoning, and put the dish to one side.

3 Cut the baguette into 1in (2.5cm) thick slices, spread the
aioli sauce on the top, cut in quarters, and place on a
baking tray in a preheated oven (300°F/150°C/Gas 2) until
the bread is dry and crispy. Leave to cool and store in an
airtight container.

FAT: 40G (61%) • PROTEIN: 3G (6%) • CARBOHYDRATE: 13G (4%)
FIBER: 1G (5%) • VITAMIN C: 20% • CALCIUM: 2% • IRON: 4% • CHOLESTEROL: 12%

The Shortcake

2 cups (300g) flour (or wheat-free)	6 tbsp soy spread
2 tbsp dark brown sugar	⅔ cup (160ml) soy milk
1 pinch of salt	2 cups (200g) blackberries
2 tsp baking powder	1¼ cups (300g) low-fat fromage frais or Quark (see *page 192*)

1 In a large bowl, mix the flour and sugar with the salt and
baking powder. Add the soy spread and mix it gently with
your fingers. Slowly add the milk to create a dough.

2 Flour the worktop and work the dough for 2 minutes.
Transfer to a cake tin and cook in a preheated oven
(400°F/200°C/Gas 6) for 15 minutes.

3 When cool, carefully split the cake in two, horizontally.
Mix the blackberries with the fromage frais and spread this
mixture between the two layers of shortcake.

FAT: 12G (19%) • PROTEIN: 12G (24%) • CARBOHYDRATE: 51G (17%)
FIBER: 2G (9%) • CALCIUM: 30% • FOLATE: 21% • CHOLESTEROL: 0

Fruit-Packed**Treat**

SERVES 4

RYE BREAD WITH HAM, CELERY, AND APPLES,
CAJUN-ROASTED POTATO WEDGES, AND
HONEY, FIG, AND NUT BAR

It's true that an apple a day really will keep the doctor away, although if you want to guarantee not to see him or her, try eating 2–3 a day for maximum health benefits. Apples have a multitude of nutritional properties. That means they can reduce cholesterol, fight bacteria and viruses, combat cancer, reduce menopausal symptoms, and boost the cardiovascular system. Full of soluble fiber, apples can also aid weight loss: eat one before a main meal to reduce your appetite. The other fruit in this healthy picnic are figs, which are not only delicious, they have also been shown to help reduce cancerous tumors.

The Potato Wedges

4 baking potatoes	**4 tbsp olive oil**
2 tsp Cajun spice	

1 Cut the potatoes into thin wedges. Toss them with the Cajun spice and the olive oil and bake on a baking sheet in a preheated oven (400°F/200°C/Gas 6) for 25–30 minutes until golden and crispy. Season to taste and eat with different dips such as hummus *(see page 126)*.

> FAT: 12G (18%) • PROTEIN: 4G (8%) • CARBOHYDRATE: 45G (15%)
> FIBER: 4G (17%) • VITAMIN C: 40% • POTASSIUM: 83% • CHOLESTEROL: 0

The Sandwich

8 slices rye bread	**1 large apple, peeled, cored, and sliced**
4 tbsp (50g) olive oil spread	**freshly ground black pepper**
4 slices cooked ham	**½ cup (100g) celery, chopped**

1 Spread the rye bread with the olive oil spread and fill your sandwiches with sliced ham, sliced apples, and celery.

> FAT: 16G (24%) • PROTEIN: 16G (32%) • CARBOHYDRATE: 39G (13%)
> FIBER: 5G (21%) • VITAMIN B$_3$: 35% • FOLATE: 17% • IRON: 15%
> CHOLESTEROL: 10%

The Honey and Fig Bar

2 tbsp soy spread	**½ tsp baking powder**
½ cup (100g) dried figs, diced	**½ cup (125ml) honey**
2 tbsp hazelnuts	**1 tsp vanilla extract**
2 tbsp pistachios	**2 eggs, beaten**
½ cup (100g) all-purpose flour (or wheat-free)	**2 tbsp peanuts**

1 Melt the soy spread and mix with the other ingredients. Line a baking sheet with waxed paper, then pour in the mixture. Spread evenly and cook in a preheated oven (350°F/180°C/Gas 4) for 20–25 minutes until it is firm to the touch and golden.
2 Leave to cool for 10 minutes, then cut into even-sized bars. When completely cold, wrap them individually and keep sealed in an airtight container.

> FAT: 12G (19%) • PROTEIN: 6G (12%) • CARBOHYDRATE: 31G (10%)
> FIBER: 4G (17%) • IRON: 10% • POTASSIUM: 29% • SELENIUM: 18%
> CHOLESTEROL: 18%

COOKING FOR HEALTHY KIDS

Polenta Pizza Faces

Proportionately, children need higher levels of carbohydrates compared with adults. A shortage causes lethargy, exhaustion, and the breakdown of proteins needed to make strong muscles in the body. As well as providing plenty of carbohydrates, these healthy pizzas are also an excellent source of calcium for growing bones, of iron, which is needed to make red blood cells and build resistance to disease, and of vitamin C, which enhances iron absorption.

MAKES 8

For the polenta base:

6 cups (1.5 liters) water

1 cup (180g) quick-cook polenta

For the tomato sauce:

2 large onions, chopped

3 garlic cloves, crushed

4 tbsp olive oil

10 medium tomatoes, skinned, deseeded, and chopped

4 tbsp tomato purée

1 pinch of sugar

2 bay leaves

1 sprig fresh oregano

freshly ground black pepper

For the faces:

½ cup (100g) mozzarella cheese, grated

16 black olives, pitted

1 red pepper, cut into strips

1 Cook the onion and garlic in the olive oil for 5 minutes, then add the other sauce ingredients. Cook gently until most of the water has evaporated.
2 Bring the water to a boil. Add the polenta and stir constantly for 7 minutes. Transfer the polenta to an oiled baking sheet (use olive oil) and leave to cool.
3 When cold, use a 2½in (6cm) round pastry cutter to cut the polenta into eight disks. Place them on a baking sheet and cover with the sauce.
4 Sprinkle over the mozzarella, then make a face with black olives for eyes and strips of red pepper for mouths. Broil until the cheese has melted and the polenta is heated through. Serve with a green salad.

> FAT: 11G (16%) • PROTEIN: 13G (44%) • CARBOHYDRATE: 48G (16%)
> FIBER: 6G (29%) • VITAMIN C: 146% • CALCIUM: 34% • IRON: 26%
> CHOLESTEROL: 2%

Homemade Bulgarian-Style Yogurt

Keep your child's heart, muscles, kidneys, and blood healthy with this simple but important dish, which is a good source of calcium and, unlike so many supermarket brands, is not processed with sugar or polluted with additives. The folate will help maintain healthy hair and skin and is also good for the nervous system. The selenium supports the pancreas and helps the body to make better use of vitamin E and build resistance to all cancers.

MAKES 4

2 cups (500ml) low-fat organic milk (use soy milk if preferred)

1 sachet of Bulgarian-style yogurt culture or similar, from your healthfood outlet

1 Bring the milk to a boil, then leave to cool until just warm. Add the yogurt culture (follow the instructions on the packet) and mix well. Sterilize a large glass bowl by pouring boiling water all over it.
2 Transfer the warm milk to the bowl, cover with plastic wrap and leave to rest for 8 hours until set. Keep in the refrigerator. Eat with the Quick Confiture of Guava (or Pineapple) *(see page 114).*

Remember to reserve one tablespoon in order to make your next batch of yogurt.

> FAT: 1.9G (3%) • PROTEIN: 6.43G (22%) • CARBOHYDRATE: 8.62G (3%)
> CALCIUM: 28% • FOLATE: 7% • POTASSIUM: 14% • SELENIUM: 13%
> CHOLESTEROL: 2%

Nutty Burgers with Tomato Sauce

This tasty meal provides at least half the recommended daily allowance of all the minerals your child needs to stay fit and well, as well as plenty of vitamin C, which regulates the normal functioning of the enzymes responsible for growth. Vitamin C also accelerates wound-healing, which is important for kids who are always "in the wars", and helps immune systems besieged by childhood bugs. This recipe is packed with iron supplies and just goes to show that choosing the right type of burgers can be a healthy choice!

SERVES 4

1 medium cauliflower, cut into florets	**1¾oz (50g) pumpkin seeds**
2 large onions, finely diced	**1¾oz (50g) sunflower seeds, roasted**
2 garlic cloves, crushed	**½ cup (100g) flour**
4 tbsp olive oil	**2 eggs, beaten**
1 tsp paprika	**½ cup (125g) breadcrumbs**
½ cup (50g) almonds, chopped	**1¾ cups (400ml) tomato sauce (see sauce recipe for Polenta Pizza Faces, page 132)**
½ cup (50g) pecans, chopped	

1 Boil the cauliflower in water until very tender. Drain well, transfer to a food processor, and blend until smooth. Cook the onion and garlic in olive oil for 10 minutes until tender, but not discolored.

2 In a large bowl, combine the cauliflower with the paprika, chopped nuts, seeds, onions, and garlic. Form into round burger shapes and coat first in the flour, then in the beaten eggs, and finally in the breadcrumbs.

3 Spread the burgers with a little olive oil on both sides, then cook them on a barbecue or griddle until golden. Serve with tomato sauce and healthy brown rice.

> FAT: 20G (29%) • PROTEIN: 11G (38%) • CARBOHYDRATE: 35G (11%)
> FIBER: 10G (48%) • VITAMIN C: 138% • FOLATE: 82% • IRON: 54%
> CHOLESTEROL: 36%

Raspberry Rice Pudding

Another calcium-rich dish for growing kids, this is also high in potassium, which helps transfer nutrients through the cell membranes. Of all grains, rice is the most easily digested and the least likely to cause allergic reactions. It can help clear psoriasis. The red raspberries in the accompanying compote are good for healthy skin, nails, bones, and teeth and can help relieve stomach upsets.

SERVES 4

1 cup (200g) short-grain pudding rice	**4 fresh mint leaves**
	For the raspberry compote:
4 cups (1 liter) organic milk (or use soy milk)	**1 cup (100g) fresh raspberries**
½ tsp vanilla extract	**2 tbsp sugar**
6 tbsp sugar	**5 tsp water**
2 egg yolks, beaten	
4 tbsp almond cream	

1 Bring some water to a boil in a large pan and cook the rice for just 3 minutes to blanch it. Drain the rice, and then boil the milk with the vanilla extract, sugar, and drained rice until all the milk has evaporated and the rice is swollen with the liquid.

2 Off the heat, stir in the beaten egg yolks and the almond cream. Stir quickly to stop the heat of the rice cooking the egg yolks. Put on one side to cool.

3 To make the compote, put all the raspberries except four in a small pan with the sugar and water. Cook gently on the stove for 10 minutes. Pour some compote into the bottom of each of four ramekin dishes and cover with the creamy rice. Leave to cool completely. Decorate with the reserved raspberries and mint leaves.

For a thicker rice pudding, increase the amount of rice you cook by ¼ cup (50g). You can also substitute caramel sauce for the compote.

> FAT: 12G (17%) • PROTEIN: 12G (40%) • CARBOHYDRATE: 56G (20%)
> FIBER: 2G (11%) • CALCIUM: 41% • FOLATE: 30% • POTASSIUM: 23%
> CHOLESTEROL: 47%

Chicken in Pastry with Green Basil Sauce

Although this recipe looks high in fat, only 19 of the 83 fat grams are saturated. The chicken is packed with iron and B vitamins and the tasty green basil sauce helps stimulate the immune system.

SERVES 4

For the chicken pastry:

3 cups (500g) whole-wheat flour

1⅓ cups (200g) white flour

1 pinch of salt

¾ cup (175g) olive oil spread

¾ cup (175g) vegetable shortening

½ cup (125ml) water

3 chicken breasts, skinless, finely diced

1 carrot, grated

1 fennel bulb, sliced

2 tbsp chicken stock

3 medium tomatoes, skinned and deseeded

freshly ground black pepper

6 tbsp mozzarella cheese, grated

1 egg yolk

For the basil sauce:

4 tbsp olive oil spread

⅓ cup (50g) flour

1 cup (250ml) chicken stock

½ cup (50g) fresh parsley, chopped

6 tbsp soy cream

5 basil leaves, chopped

1 For the pastry, sift the flours, then mix in the salt, olive oil spread, and vegetable shortening until the mixture resembles breadcrumbs. Make a well in the center and add water to make a firm paste; handle this as little as possible. Cover in plastic wrap and refrigerate for 1 hour.

2 Mix the chicken with the carrot, fennel, and chicken stock. Chop the tomatoes and add the seasoning. Roll the dough to ⅛in (3mm) thickness. Use a 7½in (19cm) pastry cutter to make four disks; divide the chicken mixture between them. Sprinkle mozzarella on top of each filling.

3 Brush the edges of each disk with water and fold over, to seal in the mixture. Place on a greased baking sheet and brush with a mix of water and egg yolk. Bake at 375°F/190°C/Gas 5 for 30–40 minutes.

4 To make the sauce, melt the spread in a pan, add the flour, and cook for 2 minutes, whisking constantly. Add the chicken stock and bring gently to a boil. Cook for another 2–3 minutes until the sauce thickens, then stir in the parsley, cream, and basil. Season and serve with vegetables and green sauce.

FAT: 83G (120%) • PROTEIN: 42G (142%) • CARBOHYDRATE: 143G (48%)
FIBER: 21G (100%) • VITAMIN B₃: 200% • VITAMIN C: 95% • FOLATE: 94%
IRON: 94% • CHOLESTEROL: 36%

Date-Stuffed Baked Apples with Honey

Tiredness, irritability, and sleeplessness are all signs of vitamin B₃ (niacin) deficiency, which this recipe combats. As well as maintaining a healthy nervous system, vitamin B₃ helps regulate hormones, and so is particularly important for teenagers. Dates, which have a delicious, natural sweetness, help keep the digestion healthy.

SERVES 4

4 large cooking apples

4 tbsp almonds, blanched and chopped

6 tbsp dried dates, chopped

4 tbsp honey

4 cloves

2 tbsp soy spread

1 Core the apples and, a third of the way down from the top, pierce the skins and make an incision, no more than ⅒in (2mm) into the flesh, around the whole circumference of each apple.

2 Arrange in a baking dish that is deep enough to hold enough water to cover the bottom ½in (1cm) of the apples. In the center of each apple, where you have removed the core, fill with almonds, dates, honey, a clove, and the soy spread, in that order. Pour warm water into the bottom of the tray.

3 Bake in a preheated oven (400°F/200°C/Gas 6) for 15 minutes. Then, turn each apple upside down, and cook for another 30–35 minutes. Serve the apples with hot custard or vanilla ice cream.

FAT: 12G (17%) • PROTEIN: 3G (10%) • CARBOHYDRATE: 63G (21%)
FIBER: 8G (39%) • VITAMIN B₃: 20% • VITAMIN C: 27% • POTASSIUM: 21%
CHOLESTEROL: 0

Popeye's Fat Jacket Potatoes

Although spinach can inhibit the full absorption of calcium, it is full of goodness and helps boost levels of other nutrients, so it should be included in some of your children's meals. In small doses, nutmeg, a very calming herb, improves the appetite, which makes it helpful for fussy eaters. Nutmeg also aids the digestion.

SERVES 4   ①②③❹⑤❻❽

4 large baking potatoes	**½ tsp nutmeg**
2 cups (300g) rock salt (not to be eaten)	**freshly ground black pepper**
2 tbsp soy spread	**1 large bunch of fresh spinach, chopped**
2 tbsp white flour	**2 cups (400g) boneless, cooked chicken meat, diced**
1¼ cups (300ml) milk	
3½ tbsp Feta cheese	
1 egg yolk, beaten	

1 Wash the potatoes and place them on a baking sheet that has been covered in rock salt. The salt absorbs the humidity, giving a crispier skin. Cook for at least 1 hour in a preheated oven (350°F/180°C/Gas 4) until the potatoes feel soft when you squeeze them.

2 Meanwhile, prepare the white sauce. Melt the soy spread, add the flour, and cook over a gentle heat for 2–3 minutes, whisking all the time. Add the milk, stirring constantly, and bring to a boil.

3 Cook for another 2–3 minutes, until the sauce thickens. Whisk to avoid lumps. Off the heat, add the Feta cheese, beaten egg yolk, and nutmeg. Season.

4 Cook the chopped spinach with a little water, stirring occasionally, until it wilts. Remove from the heat and season.

5 In a large bowl, combine the diced chicken meat, white sauce, and the wilted spinach to make the filling.

6 When the potatoes are ready, slice in half, lengthwise, scoop out all the flesh without piercing the skin, and mix with the filling. Fill each potato skin generously with this mixture. Lightly brown the tops of the potatoes under the broiler. Serve with green French beans.

FAT: 22G (32%) • PROTEIN: 41G (138%) • CARBOHYDRATE: 33G (11%)
FIBER: 4G (17%) • VITAMIN A: 141% • FOLATE: 136% • POTASSIUM: 70%
CHOLESTEROL: 55%

Chocolate and Ginger Ice Cream

The best thing about homemade ice cream is that you know exactly what has gone into it and do not have to rely on a frequently misleading label to work out either the true fat and sugar content or which horrible additives have been used. Ginger, which is very good for relieving nausea and motion sickness, stimulates all the body's tissues, is very warming, and often helps where illness is a result of poor assimilation of nutrients.

SERVES 6   ①②❹❻

5 tbsp superfine sugar	**3 squares good quality baking chocolate, grated**
6 egg yolks	**2 stems of preserved ginger, finely diced**
2 cups (500ml) soy milk	**2 vanilla pods, split in half lengthwise**

1 To make the custard, beat the sugar and egg yolks in a large bowl until they are white and fluffy. Bring the milk, grated chocolate, diced ginger, and vanilla pods to a boil and then pour gently onto the sugar and egg mixture, whisking constantly.

2 Transfer this mixture back to the pan and cook very gently, stirring with a metal spoon, until the custard coats the back of the spoon. Remove from the heat and pour into a bowl to cool.

3 Place the chilled custard in a metal container and put in the freezer. Leave it to harden, but whisk every 20 minutes until ready. When ready to eat, scoop out the ice cream and serve with chocolate flakes and (for adults) grated stem ginger on top.

FAT: 14G (20%) • PROTEIN: 6G (22%) • CARBOHYDRATE: 25G (8%)
FIBER: 3G (15%) • VITAMIN A: 14% • IRON: 37% • POTASSIUM: 23%
CHOLESTEROL: 71%

Green Risotto Galettes

This recipe, which cleverly disguises organic vegetables, is a storehouse of antioxidants—especially betacarotenes, which help prevent cancer. Betacarotenes are converted in the body to Vitamin A, which helps the body to make better use of nutrients and boosts the immune system, helping to produce antibodies. Vitamin A is needed by all the cells in the body and, as well as promoting healthy skin, nails, hair, and bones, it will speed recovery from illness.

SERVES 4

1 large onion, finely diced

2 garlic cloves, crushed

6 tbsp olive oil

1 small zucchini, grated

1 small carrot, grated

1½ cups (300g) Arborio rice

3½ cups (900ml) vegetable stock

½ cup (70g) cooked peas

2 large tomatoes, skinned, deseeded, and chopped

freshly ground black pepper

3½ tbsp fresh Parmesan cheese, grated

5 tbsp chopped fresh parsley

2 eggs, beaten

9 tbsp (80g) polenta flour

1 In a large pan, cook the diced onion and garlic in half of the olive oil for 5 minutes, until tender. Add the grated zucchini and carrots and cook for another 5 minutes.

2 Add the Arborio rice and cook for 2 minutes, stirring to coat every grain. Begin slowly to add some of the hot vegetable stock, stirring all the time.

3 After about 10 minutes, add the peas and tomatoes. Season and add the rest of the stock a ladleful at a time, stirring continuously, until the rice is cooked: it should be puffed and creamy. Now add the Parmesan cheese and the chopped parsley and leave to cool.

4 When the rice is cold, form eight small round flat cakes (like fishcakes). Dip each one in the beaten egg and roll in polenta flour. Cook the galettes in the remaining olive oil until each side is golden and the rice in the center of each cake is heated through. Serve with a green salad.

FAT: 25G (37%) • PROTEIN: 18G (60%) • CARBOHYDRATE: 85G (28%)
FIBER: 5G (25%) • VITAMIN A: 100% • VITAMIN C: 87% • CALCIUM: 32%
CHOLESTEROL: 34%

Cranberry and Raspberry Dessert

This immune-boosting dessert will give your children a blast of vitamin C to help keep coughs, colds, and other bugs at bay—and whoever imagined that a dessert could provide almost a tenth of a day's iron requirements? Cranberries can help keep the urinary tract free from infection and raspberry is a good remedy for upset stomachs.

SERVES 4

4 cups (1 liter) cranberry juice

2 envelopes agar or vegetarian gelatin

1 cup (100g) fresh raspberries

4 fresh mint leaves

1 Put the cold cranberry juice in a pan. Add the agar or vegetarian gelatin and bring to a boil gently. Cook for 3 minutes and leave to cool.

2 Divide the fresh raspberries between four individual serving glasses (keep eight back for decoration) and pour the cooled gelatin on top.

3 Leave to set in the refrigerator and, when ready, decorate with two fresh raspberries on each portion, along with the fresh mint leaves.

You can make this dessert with any clear fruit juice.

FAT: 0.5G (4%) • PROTEIN: 0.5G (1%) • CARBOHYDRATE: 41G (14%)
FIBER: 1G (3%) • VITAMIN C: 218% • IRON: 8% • POTASSIUM: 3%
CHOLESTEROL: 0

Buckwheat Pancakes Stuffed with Ham, Eggs, and Cheese

Here is a well-balanced, fun dish that the kids will love and can even learn to make themselves. With 100 percent of their daily fiber requirement, and almost the full quota of protein, it is stuffed with nutrients that help keep the whole body in tip-top health. It contains parsley, which is probably the most neglected everyday herb, but it is so powerful that it can even correct vitamin deficiencies. Parsley, which is an excellent lung tonic, is very soothing for asthma sufferers.

SERVES 4

½ cup (75g) buckwheat flour

4 tbsp white flour

1 pinch of salt

1 egg, beaten

1 cup (250ml) milk

4 tsp olive oil

For the filling:

4 eggs

4 tsp olive oil

4 slices organic ham

3oz (80g) Gruyère cheese, grated

4 tbsp chopped fresh parsley

1 To make the pancakes, sieve the flours together into a bowl with the pinch of salt, then create a well in the middle. Add the beaten egg and a little of the milk and start to stir the flour into the center. Add more milk and whisk until you have a smooth batter.

2 Heat a pancake griddle, splash in a little of the olive oil and pour in enough of the batter to cover the bottom and make the pancake. Cook on both sides until brown but not crispy. Make four pancakes this way.

3 For the filling, fry the eggs in the olive oil. Layer the filling inside the pancakes, starting with the slice of ham, then the egg, and finishing with grated cheese and chopped parsley, reserving some cheese to sprinkle on top.

4 Fold the pancakes in half and sprinkle a little more Gruyère over the top half. Cook under a hot broiler, just long enough to melt the cheese. Serve with snow peas and a broiled tomato.

FAT: 24G (35%) • PROTEIN: 29G (99%) • CARBOHYDRATE: 22G (7%)
FIBER: 2G (100%) • VITAMIN A: 30% • CALCIUM: 40% • FOLATE: 27%
CHOLESTEROL: 80%

Strawberry Fool

This summer pudding is based around strawberries, which contain lignin—a substance that can lower cholesterol levels and protect against cancer of the colon. It binds with the bile acids to remove them and is highly recommended for diabetics. Always a favorite with kids, strawberries can also protect against viruses, preventing, for example, cold sores, and are said to prevent damage to DNA—the genetic material of cells that makes us all who we are and gives children their individual tastes and characteristics.

SERVES 4

2 cups (250g) fresh strawberries

juice of 1 lemon

1¼ cups (300g) fromage frais or Quark (see page 192)

3 egg whites

½ cup (50g) confectioner's sugar, sifted

1 Wash and dry the strawberries. In a food processor, blend them with the lemon juice and fromage frais. Whisk the egg whites and just as they begin to stiffen, gradually add the sifted confectioner's sugar.

2 Gently fold this mixture into the blended strawberry mix and pour into four individual serving dishes. Leave to set in the refrigerator for an hour and serve very cold with the Honey and Fig Loaf *(see page 112)*.

FAT: 2G (17%) • PROTEIN: 7G (23%) • CARBOHYDRATE: 29G (10%)
FIBER: 4G (19%) • VITAMIN C: 56% • CALCIUM: 19% • POTASSIUM: 20%
CHOLESTEROL: 2%

POWER JUICES

The Eco-Challenger

SPROUTED ALFALFA, TOMATO, LETTUCE, AND MINT

The so-called Father of all Foods, alfalfa is packed with nutrients because its roots can travel as deep as 125 yards (125 meters) into unpolluted earth. It is rich in vitamin B_{12}, making this juice excellent for nonmeat eaters, and contains a natural fluoride to prevent tooth decay. The taste can be too sprouty for some people, hence the name of this juice. Disguise it with a splash of Worcestershire sauce if necessary. It will be worth your while, especially if you are thinning on top, because this juice stimulates hair growth. The tomatoes help flush out toxins and lower cancer rates, and their vitamin E is a valued antiaging antioxidant.

MAKES 2 X 7FL OZ (200ML) DRINKS ② ④ ⑤ ⑥ ⑧ ⑨

4 organic tomatoes
½ cup (100g) celery stalks
½ cup (100g) lettuce
4 tbsp alfalfa sprouts
handful of fresh mint leaves

Juice all the above and drink immediately while the live enzymes are still active.

VITAMIN C: 120% • VITAMIN A: 60% • IRON: 30%	
VITAMIN E: 13% • POTASSIUM: 106% • CHOLESTEROL: 0	

Ginger Boost

GINGER, BEET, CARROT, AND ECHINACEA

The lovely blood red-orange color of this energizing juice is a sign of an abundance of vitamins and minerals. Beets strengthen the immune system, and are rich in blood-building iron. Vitamin A in carrots is a cancer-fighting antioxidant that will also promote healthy skin and nails and help regulate hormones. Ginger helps to beat off chills and improves nutrient absorption. If feeling low, add echinacea, the antibacterial, antifungal herb, to fight off infection.

MAKES 2 X 7FL OZ (200ML) DRINKS ① ③ ④ ⑧

1 tsp chopped fresh ginger
6 carrots
3 raw beets
20 drops echinacea tincture (optional)

Juice all the above and drink immediately. To maintain optimum health, drink twice a week.

VITAMIN A: 1,410% • VITAMIN C: 60% • FOLATE: 33%	
POTASSIUM: 137% • IRON: 22% • CHOLESTEROL: 0	

Get-up-and-go

APPLE, CINNAMON, AND CABBAGE

An excellent tonic for the digestion, this power juice can heal inflamed tissue and will soothe the colon, stomach lining, ulcers, and heartburn. Fresh cabbage juice can protect the prostate gland and help relieve the symptoms of skin allergies and eczema. High in bone-strengthening calcium, plus vitamins A and C, this energizing drink also contains vitamin U, which can help to relieve colitis but is rapidly destroyed, so drink immediately once juiced.

MAKES 2 X 7FL OZ (200ML) DRINKS ② ③ ④ ⑥ ⑨

5 apples
½ small white cabbage
¼ tsp ground cinnamon

Juice all the above and drink immediately while the live enzymes are still active.

VITAMIN A: 6% • VITAMIN B₆: 18% • VITAMIN C: 110%	
CALCIUM: 10% • IRON: 8% • POTASSIUM: 76% • CHOLESTEROL: 0	

The Red Devil

CRANBERRY JUICE, RASPBERRY, AND PAPAYA

Cranberries reduce the acidity of urine and keep the urinary tract in men and women free from the bacteria that can cause painful and recurrent infections, including cystitis. They can also help prevent kidney stones. Raspberries provide natural pain relief and the pepsin enzyme in the papaya aids digestion by helping to break down proteins and other foods in the stomach. This drink can help guard against stomach ulcers, especially for those taking large daily doses of aspirin, a drug that can irritate the stomach lining.

MAKES 2 X 7FL OZ (200ML) DRINKS ② ④ ⑧ ⑨

1¼ cups (300ml) cranberry juice
2 cups (200g) raspberries
1 cup (200g) papaya

Blend all the above together and drink.
If you have a urinary tract infection, try to drink this every day.

VITAMIN A: 8% • VITAMIN C: 170% • FOLATE: 10% • IRON: 6% • POTASSIUM: 43%
CHOLESTEROL: 0

Tropical Fruit Smoothie

BANANA, MANGO, AND ALMOND

High in magnesium and potassium, bananas have strong antibiotic properties, can lower cholesterol, and strengthen the stomach lining. Mango is richer in cancer-fighting vitamin A than any other tropical fruit and will also help maintain healthy reproductive organs. The king of nuts, the almond is a rich source of monounsaturated fats, which keep blood cholesterol levels low. Cancer clinics tell their patients to eat at least ten a day.

MAKES 2 X 7FL OZ (200ML) DRINKS ① ② ④ ⑥ ⑧ ⑨ ⑩

2 mangoes
1 banana
1¼ cups (500ml) almond milk (or soy milk)
4 tbsp almonds, roasted and crushed

Blend all the ingredients together and drink immediately while the live enzymes are still active.

VITAMIN A: 160% • VITAMIN B3: 17% • VITAMIN C: 100% • IRON: 10%
MAGNESIUM: 31% • POTASSIUM: 83% • CHOLESTEROL: 0

Kiwi Quencher

KIWI, APPLE, AND WHITE GRAPE

In traditional Chinese medicine, Kiwifruit is one of the foods used to treat breast cancer. It has more vitamin C and zinc than oranges. Grapes are packed with potent anticancer agents and apples can help lower cholesterol, stabilize blood sugars, and keep the cardiovascular system healthy. This juice packs a huge vitamin C punch and will help alleviate stress and boost your resistance to disease.

MAKES 2 X 7FL OZ (200ML) DRINKS ① ④ ⑥ ⑧ ⑨

7oz (200g) kiwifruit
7oz (200g) sweet dessert apples
7oz (200g) white grapes, seedless

Juice all the above and drink with breakfast.

VITAMIN C: 230% • CALCIUM: 4% • IRON: 4% • POTASSIUM: 66% • ZINC: 2%
CHOLESTEROL: 0

Energy**Booster**

Energy levels are always a reflection of the quality of food you eat. To boost your energy levels, cut out refined sugars, coffee, and alcohol and identify possible food intolerances that may be depleting your energy stores. Here, the dandelion leaves in the first course encourage body cells to make more energy. The cod is rich in B vitamins—especially B_1, which helps convert the carbohydrates you eat into more energy—and the dessert is made from energy-giving, potassium-rich bananas.

DANDELION AND PANCETTA SALAD *(see page 52)*

◆

COD FILLET WITH LIMA BEAN MASH *(see page 60)*

◆

BANANA AND ROSEMARY TATIN *(see page 108)*

Immune**System**Supporter

The immune system protects the body against infection and cancer. Recurrent and chronic infections are a sign of weakened immunity and the most common cause is nutritional deficiency. Vitamin A protects the surfaces of the skin, respiratory, and gastrointestinal tracts, which are the body's first defense against invading microorganisms. Vitamin C increases the production of interferon, which boosts natural defenses. This menu is rich in these nutrients, and also contains licorice, which further boosts resistance to infection by supporting the adrenal glands.

SHIITAKE SOUP *(see page 36)*

◆

MONKFISH SCALLOPS AND OYSTERS WITH LICORICE SAUCE
(see page 62)
ROASTED CELERIAC WITH SAGE *(see page 104)*

◆

PASSION FRUIT SALAD *(see page 116)*

MENU PLANNER

Stress**Buster**

An important antioxidant that is used in tissue growth and repair, Vitamin C
also plays a crucial role in the production of antistress hormones.
In addition, it protects against the harmful effects of pollution, enhances
immunity, boosts the absorption of iron, and helps the body fight off infection.
Here, all three courses are packed with this multirole nutrient.

BROILLED MACKEREL WITH GREEN SAUCE *(see page 42)*

◆

CHICKEN PROVENÇALE *(see page 74)*
PARSNIP AND HORSERADISH MASH *(see page 100)*

◆

SUMMER HONEY AND LAVENDER CRÈME BRULÉE *(see page 113)*

Healthy**Heart**

This low-fat, low-cholesterol menu proves you can have your cake and eat it—
as long as you substitute healthy ingredients in place of the high-fat versions.
The creamy garlic soup will help reduce your risk of heart disease. You should
try to eat fish at least twice a week, and in this fish recipe, the potassium in
the sea bass will help regulate heartbeat. Being overweight increases your risk
of heart disease but the fennel side dish is a natural appetite suppressant.
The dessert is very low in cholesterol.

AIGO-BOULIDO (CREAMY GARLIC) SOUP *(see page 34)*

◆

ROASTED SEA BASS WITH LENTILS, LEEKS, AND A
WARM TOMATO VINAIGRETTE *(see page 60)*
BRAISED FENNEL *(see page 107)*

◆

RHUBARB AND PLUM TART *(see page 118)*

Colon**Cleanser**

An estimated 15 percent of the population suffer from irritable bowel syndrome (IBS). Symptoms range from abdominal pain to alternating constipation and diarrhea, excess mucus production in the colon, and nausea. The causes can include food allergies, stress, and lack of fiber. This high-fiber menu is full of nutritious ingredients that also taste delicious. You can even serve this menu to your friends.

CHICKPEA, LIME, AND CILANTRO SALAD *(see page 50)*

◆

IMAM BAYILDI (TURKISH STUFFED EGGPLANT) *(see page 92)*
BROWN RICE

◆

PINEAPPLE AND PAPAYA ICE CREAM *(see page 116)*

Bone**Up**

A diet that is high in protein, fats, and sugar can inhibit the uptake of calcium, and while good quality cuts of organic meat are an excellent source of this crucial mineral, too much meat, coupled with too many soft drinks and too many refined grain foods, will actually flush it out. The lamb is packed with phosphorous which, together with calcium and fluoride, protects against osteoporosis. Vitamin A is also important in the formation of bones and teeth. Here the yams alone provide 680 percent of the minimum recommended daily allowance and even the handful of fresh mint in the strawberry soup will further boost calcium absorption.

TARTARE OF SALMON WITH FRESH LIME JUICE *(see page 46)*

◆

COSTOLETIE D'AGNELLO AL PARMIGIANO *(see page 84)*
TIAN OF SUMMER VEGETABLES AND GLAZED YAMS
(see pages 102 and 104)

◆

STRAWBERRY SOUP WITH RED WINE *(see page 111)*

Section**Three**

EATING FOR HEALTH

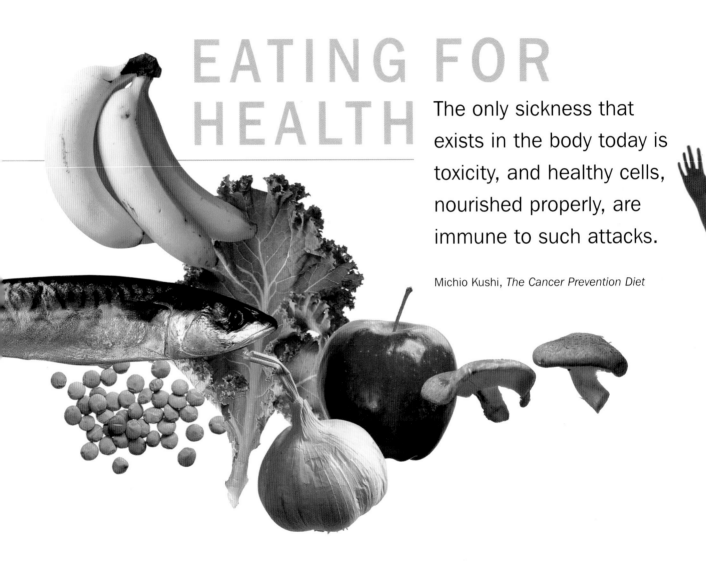

The only sickness that exists in the body today is toxicity, and healthy cells, nourished properly, are immune to such attacks.

Michio Kushi, *The Cancer Prevention Diet*

The **Immune** System

The secret of true health lies in a strong immune system, which will fight off infection, orchestrate the body's healing processes, and even regulate the rate at which you age. A strong immune system is vital: deaths from infectious diseases in the US and the UK have doubled in the last decade, one in three people suffer from allergies (a sign of weakened immunity), and cancer rates are on the rise.

The outward signs of a weakened immune system are easy to see.

There are plenty of signs that warn of impaired immunity, and you don't have to be a doctor to recognize any of them. Fatigue, lethargy, repeated infections, slow wound-healing, allergies, chronic diarrhea, yeast infections, and inflammation are all easy-to-spot clues. They prove, too, that weakening the body's defense mechanisms leaves it vulnerable to virtually every type of illness and disease.

The immune system is both complex and fascinating, and there is a delicate balance between a strong, healthy system and an overpowering one that can itself cause disease. It is possible to become ill if your immune response is too strong or directed at the wrong target. Many disorders, including allergies, lupus, pernicious anemia, rheumatoid arthritis, and even diabetes have all been linked to an inappropriate immune response. This can happen when the immune system fails in its primary task—to recognize the difference between harmless cells and chemicals and foreign or dangerous substances.

The immune system is not just one organ or even a group of organs. It is a highly organized system of various organs, systems, and cells, including white blood cells, bone marrow, and the lymphatic vessels and their organs, which all interact in a complex way. The immune system also involves specialized cells in different body tissues and specialized substances, called serum factors, that are present in the blood.

There are two types of immunity, known as innate and adaptive. Innate immunity, which is present at birth, is the first line of defense against micro-organisms. The skin, for example, naturally secretes mucus to keep out unwanted germs, while the stomach produces acid for the same job. Adaptive immunity is acquired, either through immunization or after you have successfully fought off an infection: what fascinates immunologists is how your immune system remembers every invader it has faced since you took your first breath.

Think of the immune system as an army made up of different regiments with their own jobs to do. This is how it works.

THE LYMPHATIC SYSTEM

About one-sixth of the body is made up of the space between the cells. This is known as the interstitium, and fluid within it is called the interstitial fluid. It is this fluid that flows through the lymphatic vessels to become the lymph. The lymphatic vessels, which drain waste products from the tissues, run in parallel to the arteries and veins. They take the lymph to the lymph nodes to be filtered. In the lymph nodes, important cells called macrophages engulf and destroy foreign particles, including microorganisms and cell debris. The lymph nodes also contain white blood cells which, when a foreign invader is detected, fire into action to make the antibodies that will protect the body.

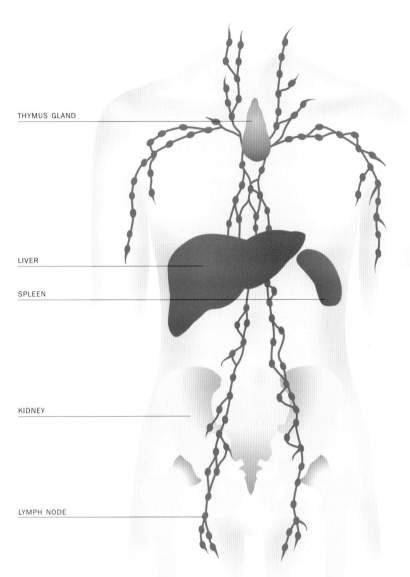

THYMUS GLAND

LIVER

SPLEEN

KIDNEY

LYMPH NODE

Fighting the Common Cold

The common cold is a general inflammation of the mucous membranes of the respiratory passages. Highly contagious, it can be caused by a variety of viruses. Healthy adults should suffer no more than two colds a year because the immune system remembers strains it has fought off and produces antibodies to protect the body. However, new generations of viruses crop up each year and even old ones can easily trick the body's defenses, because even the slightest change to a virus's chemical makeup will help it through your body's first line of defense. Poor nutrition, which weakens the immune system, is the most widespread cause of colds. If you have more than two colds a year you definitely need to support your immune system. To prevent a cold, take vitamin C with the bioflavonoid quertin on a regular basis, and at the first sign of infection take zinc. Eat foods that are rich in vitamin B_6, to boost the production of the antibodies that fight infection.

The body's frontline defense, the immune system protects against harmful substances and microorganisms. Bacteria and cell debris are detected in the lymph system and are destroyed by specialized cells produced in the lymph nodes and in the spleen. The whole system is orchestrated by the thymus gland, which also produces specialized cells, called T-cells, to destroy invading bacteria.

The **Immune** System

THE ORGANS

The thymus gland, which lies just above the heart, controls much of the body's immune function. It secretes hormones that regulate the immune system and produces T-lymphocytes, (T-cells—see illustration below) which are another form of white blood cell. When immunity is dangerously impaired, the level of T-cells in the body drops. The spleen is the largest mass of lymphatic tissue in the body. The size of a fist, it lies in the upper left abdomen behind the lower ribs and works hard to produce white blood cells and destroy bacteria and cellular debris. It mops up and destroys old blood cells and acts as the body's blood bank.

SPECIALIZED SERUM FACTORS

When specialists talk about immunity, you hear them mention the terms interferon and interleukin II. These are chemicals produced by the various white blood cells. T-cells produce interferon and macrophage cells produce interleukin. These substances help enhance immunity and are called serum factors. They activate the white blood cells to seek out and destroy cancer cells and viruses.

IMMUNE BOOSTERS

Stress takes its toll on the immune system by increasing the production of fight-or-flight hormones, including adrenaline, which, in turn, depress the activity of white blood cells and cause the thymus gland to shrink. The more prolonged the stress, the greater the damage to the immune system.

To counter this vicious circle, make sure you get plenty of good quality sleep (important immune-enhancing compounds are released during sleep) and practice meditation. Your immunity gradually declines with age, but overwork, sleeplessness, and prolonged stress will accelerate the rate of decline.

DIET

To support your immune system, each day your diet needs to include 3–5 servings of fruit and vegetables, a heaped teaspoon of seeds (sunflower or pumpkin), a clove of garlic, and eight glasses of water. You should drink herbal teas and fruit juices in preference to coffee and tea and eat shiitake mushrooms three times a week, unless you have a fungal infection (*see pages 36 and 44 for shiitake recipes*). Reduce the amount of sugar

Natural-born Killers

Forget about the movie: the Natural Killer Cells (NKC) are the Marine Corps of your system. They destroy cells that have become cancerous or infected by viruses and are the body's first line of defense against cancer. They work with T-cells (left) to fight disease by destroying cancerous cells. The levels and activity of these important cells are low in people who suffer from Chronic Fatigue Syndrome, cancer, and any kind of chronic viral infection. To increase the activity of your Natural Killer Cells, stop smoking, eat more green vegetables, eat regular meals, and maintain a healthy body weight. Make sure you get more than seven hours of sleep each night, exercise regularly, eat a vegetarian diet, and get tested for any nutritional deficiencies, which you can then reverse with supplements.

*Seeds from sunflowers
can boost immunity.*

in your diet (eat less than 2 tablespoonfuls a day)
and cut out alcohol. Studies of human white
blood cells show they are much slower to
mobilize to areas of infection in those who have
consumed even a modest amount of alcohol. High
cholesterol levels can also stop white blood cells
from getting to infected sites and slow down the
rate at which they multiply. Vitamin A promotes
thymus health and can prevent the organ from
shrinking. It also maintains the surfaces of the
skin, respiratory and gastrointestinal tracts,
which, when healthy, act as a barrier to
microorganisms. Natural sources of vitamin A
include yellow fruits and vegetables, organic
milk, and eggs. Vitamin C will enhance immune
response by increasing the production of white
blood cells and interferon. Citrus fruits, broccoli,
kale, peas, tomatoes, orange juice,
guava, papaya, and Kiwifruit are all
excellent food sources of vitamin C.

SUPPLEMENTS

To keep your immune system strong, take a good
multivitamin containing at least 10,000 IUs
(international units) of vitamin A, 150mg of
vitamin E, 25–50mg of B vitamins, 200–400mg
of calcium and magnesium, 10mg of zinc,
and 50mcg of selenium. In addition, take
1–3g a day of immune-boosting vitamin C
and an antioxidant supplement so that you
are taking a daily total of 20,000 IUs of
vitamin A and betacarotene, 150mg of vitamin
E, 15mg of zinc, and 100mcg of selenium.

*Eating plenty of garlic,
shiitake mushrooms, citrus
fruit, and broccoli will
keep your immune system
in peak condition,
providing plenty of
antioxidant vitamins A and
C as well as other
antiviral, protective
substances.*

HERBS

Lots of herbs have a potent effect on the immune system. The bestselling
immune herb is echinacea (*see page 19*), which activates the macrophage
white blood cells. It is also an antibacterial and antiviral agent, but should
only be used in the short term. In Chinese medicine, astragalus
root is used to treat viral infections. It appears to work well where
the immune system has been damaged by chemicals or radiation.

*The root and leaves of the echinacea plant have long
been valued as a support for the immune system.*

The **Digestive** System

The saying "You are what you eat" is well known, but many health practitioners qualify it by saying "You are what you *absorb*." The process of digestion is complicated and involves many different organs and chemical processes. Many people eating a traditional Western diet have a dysfunctional digestive system, meaning that they do not absorb all the nutrients they need from their food.

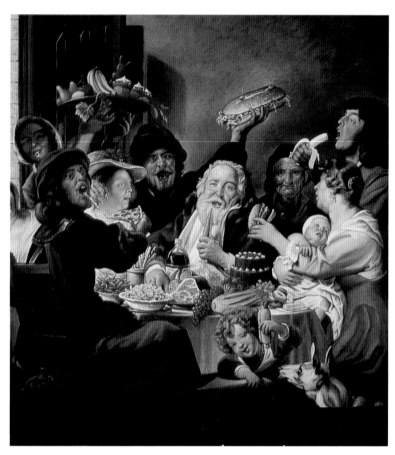

Throughout history, food has always been a major part of any celebration as this picture by Hess shows.

You will not get the full benefit of any of the nutrients you eat—either from your diet or from supplements—if your digestive tract does not work properly. Naturopaths estimate that 70 percent of all diseases are caused or exacerbated by problems in the gut. While maintaining good colon health is as simple as eating a high-fiber diet, drinking plenty of water, and maintaining a healthy balance of microflora in the gut, many of us struggle to digest and eliminate our food properly. In the US, over 4 million people frequently suffer from constipation. In the UK, Irritable Bowel Syndrome (IBS), which causes alternating constipation and diarrhea, is now believed to be responsible for as many days off sick as back pain.

The main function of your digestive system is to break down the food you eat so that your body can absorb the nutrients it needs and flush out those that are surplus to requirements. This process, which is both chemical and mechanical, starts in the mouth, where the saliva contains special enzymes that begin the process of breaking food down. The simple act of chewing signals to all the other gastrointestinal components to swing into action ready for digestion.

Once your food has been sufficiently chewed, it is transported to the stomach, which churns it up and mixes it with the digestive juices. Food does not leave the stomach until it is in a semiliquid state, which is called chyme. This then moves into the 21ft (7m) long small intestine, where the minerals are absorbed first, followed by the carbohydrates and proteins. Finally, in the last section of the small intestine, fat, cholesterol, and the bile salts that aid digestion are absorbed.

Both highly complex and truly integrated, the digestive system runs from the mouth to the anus, involving, along the way, the salivary glands, the liver, the gallbladder, and the pancreas. Since it also controls the elimination of waste and toxins, when the digestive system is sluggish or goes wrong, as well as causing internal problems, it can adversely affect the condition of your skin, hair, and nails, and can even cause acne. It can also exacerbate a variety of other ailments, including arthritis and hemorrhoids.

DYSBIOSIS

In a normal gut, there are more than 3lb (1kg) of bacteria, including so-called "friendly" bacteria as well as harmful ones. Some health practitioners believe that the balance may be thrown out, leading to a condition called dysbiosis, which can accelerate the onset of conditions such as IBS.

Typically, the beneficial bacteria are outnumbered by those that can cause problems. At best, the good bacteria make up only a third of the population of microflora in the intestines. At worst, especially after the prolonged use of antibiotics or after years of a diet high in refined foods and sugar, levels of friendly bacteria may be so low they are virtually undetectable.

With dysbiosis, there are so few beneficial bacteria populating the gut that numbers of the pathogenic bacteria, such as *Escherichia coli*, which make unhealthy byproducts are allowed to

Good Guys, Bad Guys

The good guys are the bifidobacteria (left). When present in sufficient quantities in the gut, they help lower cholesterol levels, prevent food poisoning, alleviate constipation, and help the body to digest lactose (the sugar in milk) and to manufacture important B vitamins, including folic acid, which is now believed to protect against heart disease. These bacteria also prevent diarrhea and produce chemicals that alter the acidity of the gut, making it harder for the "bad guy" bacteria (right) to flourish.

flourish and increase to dangerously high levels.

Conditions believed by some to stem from dysbiosis include acne, Chronic Fatigue Syndrome (*see page 174*), Irritable Bowel Syndrome, food allergies (*see page 168*), depression (*see page 178*), Candida (yeast infections), rheumatoid arthritis, and colitis.

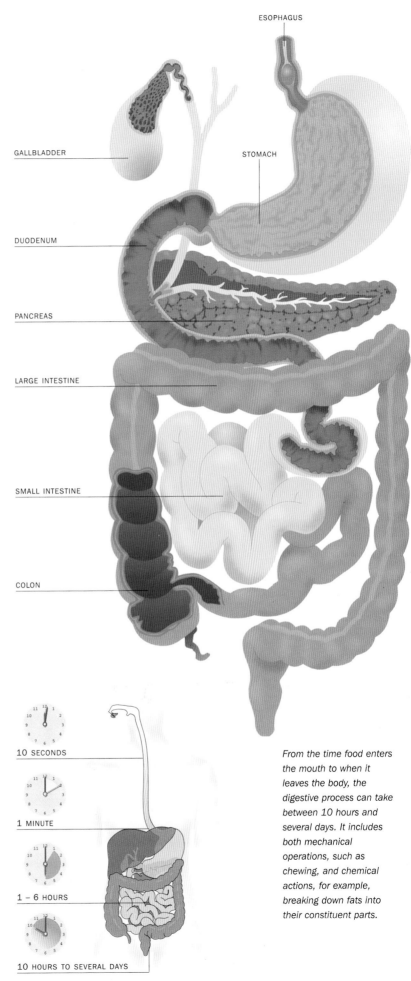

ESOPHAGUS

GALLBLADDER

STOMACH

DUODENUM

PANCREAS

LARGE INTESTINE

SMALL INTESTINE

COLON

10 SECONDS

1 MINUTE

1 – 6 HOURS

10 HOURS TO SEVERAL DAYS

From the time food enters the mouth to when it leaves the body, the digestive process can take between 10 hours and several days. It includes both mechanical operations, such as chewing, and chemical actions, for example, breaking down fats into their constituent parts.

The **Digestive** System

Foods such as bananas, honey, asparagus, artichokes, and tomatoes are all rich natural sources of FOS, which has probiotic properties, meaning that it feeds the friendly bacteria in the gut.

in Japan. Although FOS taste sweet, like sugar, in the body they act like fiber because they have a molecular structure which passes, undigested, from the stomach into the large intestine.

Once there, FOS act as a nourishing food for the beneficial gut bacteria that, when flourishing, help the body to make protein, assist the digestion and absorption of nutrients, and support the immune system in its work to fight infection and prevent harmful bacteria from multiplying.

FOS occur naturally in foods such as bananas, onions, garlic, artichokes, barley, tomatoes, rye, honey, and asparagus, but while eating these foods on a regular basis will help you maintain healthy digestion, if you already have digestive problems, you would have to eat them by the bucketful to get a significant therapeutic dose. Fortunately, supplementation is simple. FOS is sold either as a powder or a syrup. For maximum benefit, the brand you buy should be at least 95 percent pure. If you are not sure what you are buying, check with the manufacturer. Adults can take 1g a day.

If you suffer from any of the conditions just mentioned, you need to investigate natural ways to repopulate your intestine with friendly microflora.

Lots of people know that eating natural yogurt can help with this. What they don't know is that for the yogurt to provide any beneficial bacteria it must be live and very few labels will tell you exactly which strain of bacteria you are eating. To tackle ailments caused by a disrupted digestive tract, you need to consult a nutritionist to make sure you get not only optimal amounts of these bacteria but exactly the right strains.

PROBIOTIC FOODS

The widespread problem of dysbiosis has led to much interest in substances called fructooligosaccharides, whose tongue-twister of a name is, thankfully, always shortened to FOS. The first of the new so-called "functional foods" that have been engineered to promote health in a specific way, they are a complex sugar derived from plants and already used in around 500 foods

DIET AND BOWEL FUNCTION

Ailments that may be caused by prolonged constipation include diverticulosis, hemorrhoids, hernias, boils, bowel cancer, cellulite, indigestion, bloating, obesity, varicose veins, headaches, insomnia, halitosis, and gas. The continued use of commercial laxatives is not the answer, because far from relieving the problem, they simply perpetuate it, often leading to physical dependence. Chemical laxatives work by stimulating the bowel nerves and this eventually weakens the muscles. A healthier alternative is to add fiber-rich ground psyllium seeds to your food and drink plenty of water. Avoid dairy products which, being mucus-forming, only make the problem worse. In addition, get regular, moderate exercise to encourage the movement of waste through the intestines and prevent the accumulation of toxins, which, if not eliminated, will make you sick.

If you do suffer from constipation, eating extra bran may exacerbate the problem, especially if the lining of your gut has been stripped of friendly bacteria by antibiotics or other conventional

Chamomile tea soothes the digestive tract.

wholegrains, soy products, dark-green leafy vegetables, and nuts.

The most frequent cause of diarrhea is the presence of bacteria that are alien to the digestive tract. These usually come from food poisoning, or eating food that has been poorly refrigerated, undercooked, or is partially rancid. Diarrhea can also be caused by prolonged use of laxatives, emotional stress, food allergies, heavy drinking, too much caffeine, infection, pancreatic problems, prescription drugs, and parasites. If you have diarrhea, avoid milk products, which will make it worse. When you have recovered, eat foods that are particularly rich in nutrients, such as wheat germ and watercress, as well as foods that can help to restore healthy gut flora, such as natural yogurt or sauerkraut.

HERBS

Herbs that help restore normal digestive function include ginger (especially useful if you have stomach cramps), chamomile, agrimony, and goldenseal, which is a powerful antibacterial agent.

Detox Plan

The best way of flushing toxins and wastes from the body is a fast, which is usually the first step in any colon-cleansing program. To detoxify your system, drink the juice of a fresh lemon squeezed into a cup of warm water both first thing in the morning and last thing at night. The herb pau d'arco will help restore the acid/alkaline balance of the colon and promote healing. It tastes very "plantish," but has excellent detoxifying properties and is also useful in treating persistent Candida (yeast) infection.

drug ... s of people step u ... t by increa ... ey forget to increas ... k in proporti ...

Aloe v ... ged gut lining, bu ... manufactu ... buy is high in the ... and heal the lini ... glass in the mornir ... which is a goc ... tly stimulate the c ... day if you suffer fro ...

Magnesium, ... function, is frequ ... diets—in fact mag...sium deficiency is the second most common deficiency in both men and women. Good natural sources include seafood,

For a healthy bowel, eat plenty of magnesium-rich foods such as fish, shrimp and other seafood, brown rice, and spinach.

Skin
Disorders

They may not be life-threatening, but skin conditions such as acne, psoriasis and eczema cause much distress to sufferers and can be notoriously difficult to eradicate completely. However, new research is revealing that diet plays an unexpectedly important part in skin problems and sufferers can help themselves by adopting a healthy diet, supplemented where necessary with vital minerals and vitamins.

The skin is not just a protective wrapping—it is the body's largest organ. As well as regulating body temperature and sensing both painful and pleasant stimuli, it shields us from the harmful effects of the sun and prevents many substances, including microorganisms, from entering the body, and so is our first true line of defense. Many skin disorders can be diagnosed just by looking at them, yet dermatology remains medicine's poor relation and a significant number of skin diagnoses turn out to be wrong.

HAIR

EPIDERMIS

BLOOD VESSEL

DERMIS

HAIR ERECTOR
(MUSCLE)

The skin is the body's first line of defense and is an important excretory organ.

ACNE

The most common of all skin disorders, acne is becoming more prevalent in adults. Characterized by the recurring formation of blackheads, whiteheads, and pimples (mostly on the face but sometimes on the shoulders, chest, and back, too), it is caused not by junk diets or poor hygiene but by hormones and bacterial infection.

Pimples form close to the surface of the skin pore when the cells that line the hair canal produce an excess of keratin—the fibrous protein that is the main component of the outermost layer of skin. This keratin begins to block the canal, forming a blackhead if the blockage is only partial, and a whitehead if the blockage is total. A bacterium called *Propionibacterium acnes* (*P. acnes*) starts to overgrow and releases the enzymes that cause the painful and unsightly inflammation.

Most people think acne is caused by too much of the male hormone, testosterone, but new research suggests that the problem is not one of increased testosterone levels, but, more accurately, is one of how the skin metabolizes this hormone. The skin of acne sufferers has now been found to exhibit greater activity of an enzyme called 5-alpha-reductase that converts testosterone to a more potent form called dihydrotestosterone (DHT).

Intestinal health also plays a role in acne: in one study, 50 percent of patients with severe acne had increased blood levels of toxins absorbed from the gut. Yet doctors persist in prescribing antibiotics for acne. Why? In many cases, the *P. acnes* bacterium has become resistant to any antibiotic treatment and, as well as being ineffective in such cases, the prolonged use of antibiotics will almost certainly upset the delicate balance of the microflora in your digestive tract.

Foods that help those prone to acne include nuts and shellfish, which are rich sources of zinc. Bananas are beneficial, helping to restore levels of friendly bacteria in the gut, and broccoli is an excellent plant source of calcium, which acne sufferers lack.

HOW TO HELP

A low-salt, calcium-rich diet can help. So will vitamin A, which helps maintain the surface of the skin, and zinc, which is an efficient antibacterial agent. Calcium-rich foods include green leafy vegetables, organic dairy products, broccoli, tofu, and shellfish. Natural good sources of vitamin A include yellow fruits and vegetables and fish from unpolluted waters. Rich sources of zinc include wheat germ, peanuts, shellfish, pecans, and turkey. Bananas can help repopulate the good bacteria in the gut, but for severe infections, probiotic FOS supplements are recommended.

ROSACEA

A chronic skin disorder in which the cheeks and nose are abnormally flushed and covered in acne-like eruptions, rosacea is more common in women than men. It affects adults aged between 30 and 50 and, although no cause has been identified as yet, sufferers have been found to lack B vitamins, especially B_2 (riboflavin), which not only energizes cells, but works within them to clear out toxins.

Gastrointestinal disorders may also be to blame, with insufficient hydrochloric acid in the stomach—a condition called hypochlorhydria—frequently cited as a contributing factor.

Skin Disorders

Foods such as almonds, meat, fish, and yogurt are all good sources of vitamin B2, which research has shown that people with rosacea lack. Drinking fennel tea helps ease rosacea by flushing toxins out of the system.

Hydrochloric acid helps to break down nutrients in the stomach. Too little can impair the absorption of vitamins and minerals and can affect the digestion of protein.

HOW TO HELP

If you suffer from rosacea, avoid hot drinks and spicy foods, which may exacerbate the skin's flush reaction, and apply tea tree oil to the rash. Eliminate refined sugars, fried foods, and anything that contains trans-fatty acids, including margarine and synthetically hydrogenated vegetable oils. Supplement your diet with a good B-complex vitamin and eat plenty of foods rich in riboflavin (vitamin B_2) such as cheese, chicken, organic milk and yogurt, fish, pork, almonds, and organ meats. Brewers' yeast and wheat germ are also rich in B_2. A probiotic, such as acidophilus, and digestive enzymes can both help compensate for the low levels of hydrochloric acid. Herbs that may help include chamomile and fennel—drink these as herbal teas.

ECZEMA

Characterized by chronically itchy and inflamed skin that becomes very red, dry, and scaly, eczema, or atopic dermatitis, is believed to affect up to 7 percent of the population. It is becoming increasingly common among children and, while sufferers spend a fortune on topical creams, most patients will improve on a diet that eliminates the most common food allergens. In children, allergies to milk, eggs, and peanuts account for over 80 percent of eczema cases. These allergies are believed to create "leaky gut," a condition in which the consequence of increased permeability of the intestinal lining is an overburdened immune system that has to deal with food molecules that would not normally have penetrated through the lining of the stomach.

In adults with eczema, low zinc levels may also play a role. There is usually a family history of the condition and most sufferers go on to develop asthma and/or hay fever. There is also a direct link between eczema and a compromised immune system, so any measure that boosts the body's natural defenses will help. Sample white blood cells taken from the skin of patients with eczema, for example, have been shown to have an abnormality that causes them to release higher amounts of histamine and other allergic compounds. An overgrowth of the common yeast, *Candida albicans*, has also been linked with eczema.

HOW TO HELP

The successful treatment of eczema requires a two-pronged approach. You need to reduce the burden on the immune system by cutting out known allergenic substances and you also need to prevent the body's tendency to release histamine and other allergic factors in the skin. Through a process of elimination, identify the foods you are allergic to and avoid them for at least a year. Research has shown that in many cases, not eating the offending food for 12 months effectively robs it of its potency and the sufferer appears to outgrow the allergy. Next, replace animal products with fatty fish, especially salmon, mackerel, herring, and halibut. Take zinc and vitamin A and E

People with eczema benefit from a diet based around zinc-rich fish and shellfish. They should avoid milk, milk products, and peanuts.

supplements and substitute tea, coffee, and sugary soft drinks with green tea, three times a day. Licorice can also help (*see page 62 for a zinc-rich fish and licorice recipe*).

PSORIASIS

In 50 percent of psoriasis cases, there is a family history of the condition. Psoriasis affects men and women equally and generally first appears in the late twenties. As well as affecting the skin, causing a red rash covered with overlapping silvery scales, it can also cause an inflammatory form of arthritis.

The areas most often affected are the scalp, the back of the wrists, the elbows, knees, buttocks, and ankles. Caused by a basic defect in the skin, the cells replicate too quickly to be shed properly. They replicate 1,000 times faster than normal skin, and it is the resulting accumulation of cells that produces the characteristic silvery scales.

The rate at which cells divide is controlled by a delicate balance between two compounds: cyclic adenosine monophosphate (AMP) and cyclic guanidine monophosphate (GMP). Higher than normal levels of GMP cause cells to divide too fast.

Higher levels of AMP reduce the rate of cell replication. Bizarrely, studies also show a drop in the levels of both AMP and GMP causes the cells to divide too fast again, so a correct balance between these compounds and normal levels of both are crucial for cells to divide at the usual rate.

Other factors that either cause or contribute to psoriasis include poor protein digestion, bowel toxemia, impaired liver function, too much alcohol, too much saturated animal fat in the diet, nutritional deficiencies, and stress.

HOW TO HELP

Making efforts to stop overburdening the liver is a good first step. Cut out alcohol, which has definitively been linked with psoriasis, and drink organic nettle tea, which is an excellent liver tonic. Fish oils, which are rich in the omega-3 fatty acids, have been shown to improve psoriasis significantly. Following a gluten-free diet with plenty of fiber can also help, and so can plenty of sunlight. Decreased levels of both vitamin A and zinc have been identified among sufferers and there is growing evidence that vitamin D plays an important role in cell replication. Natural food sources of vitamin D include salmon, mackerel, tuna, and egg yolks.

As well as avoiding alcohol, people with psoriasis should increase their vitamin D intake with plenty of oily fish and eggs. Nettle tea helps to cleanse the system.

Cold Sores

Caused by the herpes simplex virus, which invades and reprograms healthy cells, cold sores are an unsightly condition. The good news, however, is that the immune system eventually becomes more efficient at suppressing the virus. If you have cold sores, eat foods high in the amino acid lysine, which has been shown to slow the growth of this virus. These include fish, shellfish, fruit, vegetables, legumes, and brewers' yeast. Avoid flour, sugar, soft drinks, coffee, alcohol, and processed foods. During an outbreak, do not eat foods that contain the amino acid L-arginine. These include chicken, cereals, almonds, and chocolate. Some citrus fruits may also exacerbate the infection.

Allergies and Intolerance

True allergies provoke anaphylactic shock: a life-threatening, but thankfully rare, severe reaction of the immune system to certain drugs, food substances, or insect stings. Food intolerances are much less dramatic, but far more common. Many health practitioners believe that they are a growing problem and that they are an underlying factor in disorders ranging from headaches and digestive problems to depression and chronic fatigue syndrome.

Pollen, shown magnified here, can provoke an allergic reaction.

The housedust mite feeds on dust and dead skin.

Close-up view of a long-eared owl's feather.

Allergies are triggered when susceptible individuals are exposed to common allergens such as pollen, animal dander (particles of skin and feathers), and the housedust mite.

Dog skin and hair seen through a microscope.

The word "allergy" simply means altered reactivity. It refers to any inappropriate response by the immune system to a substance that is not usually harmful. When your body mistakenly identifies a harmless food, for example, as a toxic invader, the immune system goes into overdrive to produce an abundance of histamine, which increases blood flow in the capillaries supplying the membranes. This then causes swelling and congestion. The body's white blood cells start to overreact too and end up doing more damage than the offending substance.

When this happens, the allergic response itself has become a condition, the symptoms of which can include coughing, wheezing, nasal congestion, itching, headache, fatigue, hay fever, asthma, eczema, high blood pressure, constipation, dizziness, nausea, abnormal tiredness, urticaria, and other skin rashes.

Substances that provoke an allergic response are called allergens. The most common ones are pollen, dust, animal hair, certain metals, food additives, and chemicals in household soaps, detergents, and washing powders.

Food, too, can provoke an allergic response. The most common offenders are chocolate, peanuts, dairy products, eggs, shellfish, strawberries, and wheat. If you are allergic to these, the reaction is so severe that you will already know about it. However, a major allergy can often mask a minor one and when you clear the main problem, you may still be plagued by an allergy to foods you had thought you could tolerate.

ALLERGY OR INTOLERANCE?

It is important to make the distinction between a food allergy and a food intolerance. In an allergy, the immune system generates an antibody response to the allergen. Food intolerance on the other hand is the inability to digest and process certain foods correctly and is usually caused by a lack of certain digestive enzymes. Food intolerance can, though, lead to a food allergy if undigested particles of food enter the bloodstream where they can cause an allergic reaction.

If you are highly allergic to certain foods, you will already know all about it. You may have a dramatic allergic response as soon as you start chewing the food and will have already eliminated it from your diet. If your reaction is not as extreme, you may suspect you are allergic to one of the foods you eat more than twice a week. For most people, the most common offenders are likely to be wheat, eggs, citrus fruit, dairy products, tea, and coffee. Choose one of these and exclude it from your diet for six days. (If you're testing a number of foods, test them individually and make sure you have a week of rest between testing different substances.) To help you keep track of your reactions and what you are testing, keep a food diary. Also, remember if you are allergic to one member of a particular food group, you are likely to react in the same way to

Some of the most common foods that trigger allergies include strawberries, chocolate, shellfish and eggs.

other members of that group. For example, if you react to potatoes, you may also react in the same way to tomatoes, peppers, and eggplants (all part of the *Solanaceae* family).

When you embark on allergy testing through elimination, you can expect to feel worse before you feel better. You may have headaches or even flu-like symptoms. These are a good sign—they show you are definitely sensitive to the food you have just eliminated.

In healthy people, the lining of the intestine generates new cells faster than any other tissue in the body. When they work properly, these cells make a permeable lining that acts as a filter, allowing the nutrients we need to pass through, but blocking those nutrients and toxins that will cause an allergic response if they get into the bloodstream. The lining can do this because it is full of tiny holes. Damage to the intestinal lining can increase the size of these holes and cause a condition known as "leaky gut" in which toxins and foods that should not pass into the blood get through the filter, prompting the immune system to mount an allergic-reaction type of attack.

If left unchecked, a leaky gut can even cause the body's natural defenses to mistake your own body tissue for a foreign invader that they then begin to destroy.

If you meticulously write down everything you eat for a week in a food diary, you will be able to work out what triggers your food intolerances.

Allergies and Intolerance

Test Yourself

Some doctors believe that at least 60 percent of Americans suffer symptoms linked to some form of food intolerance. To test yourself for an allergic reaction, relax and then measure your pulse rate. You should count 52–70 beats a minute, which is the sign of a healthy pulse. Now eat the food you want to test. Wait 15–20 minutes and take your pulse rate again. If it has increased by more than 10 beats per minute, eliminate it from your diet for a month and then retest. When testing any food in this way, always try to eat the food in its purest form. The elimination and reintroduction of a food is the most foolproof way of pinpointing the substances causing an allergic reaction. Allergies run in families, but you can break the cycle if you stop eating the offending food for a minimum of two years. You must be strict about this and when you do reintroduce it, don't eat it more than once every five days or you will have an adverse reaction again.

When the immune system is confused in this way, it will cause an autoimmune disease, a problem that some believe to be at the root of many conditions, including inflammatory bowel disease and arthritis. In trials, children and adults suffering from eczema and asthma that was triggered by food allergy were found to have higher gut permeability. To help repair a "leaky" gut, avoid the foods to which you are sensitive (*see* Test Yourself, *above*).

Tomatoes, eggplants, potatoes, and peppers belong to the same plant family. If you are allergic to one, you may be allergic to them all.

HOW TO HELP

The number of adults and children who suffer from food intolerances has increased dramatically in recent years. There are three reasons for this. First, most of us regularly eat too much of a limited number of foods—if you eat the same foods every day, your body gradually becomes intolerant of them. Second, there are high levels of artificial colorings, preservatives, flavorings, and stabilizers now added to food, which exacerbate the problem. Third, impaired digestion as a result of a leaky gut is also partially to blame.

To avoid an allergic reaction, first identify and stop eating the foods you know you react to. Food allergies often develop slowly, so in addition rotate the foods you eat, and don't eat the same food more than once every four days. For example, if you eat fish on Friday, wait at least until Tuesday before eating fish again. Rotating foods not only makes you feel better, it will encourage you to be more adventurous in the kitchen and cook with foods that are new to you.

Nettle and Sorrel soup (*see page 34*), for example, can both help relieve inflammation and clear congestion. It contains vitamin C, which the body needs to help it cope with the overproduction of histamine that results from an allergic response. The soup is also rich in B vitamins, which helps ease allergic symptoms.

Try eating foods rich in quercetin, a bioflavonoid that has been found to stabilize cell membranes, stopping them from seeping histamine into the surrounding blood and tissue. Good natural sources include red onions, shallots, squash, zucchini, and broccoli. Quercetin, which is also sold as a supplement, is even more effective when teamed with bromelain, an enzyme found in pineapple that has excellent anti-inflammatory properties and which, incidentally, can help prevent cold sores.

The omega-3 fatty acids found in fish oils and other substances contain potent anti-inflammatory compounds, so if you have an allergic response, eat plenty of salmon, mackerel, and flaxseed oil.

Herbs can help prevent an allergic attack. Echinacea supports the immune system, the Chinese herb ginkgo has been shown to be

A diet rich in vegetables such as squash, zucchini, and broccoli, with plenty of oily fish and pineapple will reduce the sensitivity of the gut and provide vital nutrients for those suffering from food allergies and intolerances.

effective in treating the bronchial constrictions that are typical of an asthma attack prompted by an allergy, and eyebright, as its name suggests, is good for relieving itchy eyes.

You should avoid foods containing additives and colorings, and choose organic whenever possible. In the last 50 years, there has been an explosion in the number of new chemicals in daily use in farming and the environment and many of these find their way into the human body.

Sensitivity to chemicals is believed to be a growing problem: for example,

Ginkgo, the oldest species of tree on the planet, contains anti-inflammatory chemicals that help reduce the severity of an allergic reaction.

many of those who suffer from Chronic Fatigue Syndrome overreact to chemicals. Also, Multiple Chemical Sensitivity (MCS), which is not yet recognized by conventional medicine, has been described by complementary practitioners as the most puzzling disease of the new century. Symptoms range from headaches and depression to flu-like ailments, gastric problems, and joint pains. The main culprits appear to be pesticides—particularly organophosphates—which can accumulate in fat. It certainly makes sense to avoid food grown using intensive farming methods since we cannot remain infinitely tolerant of new chemicals that are being pumped into the body.

Finally, there is no simple cure for allergies and they are always worse when you are under stress, so try to control the severity of an attack by learning some form of relaxation technique and practicing it every day.

The **Heart** and **Blood**

The number one killer in both the US and the UK, heart disease accounts for more than 40 percent of all deaths in the States. We expect so much from our heart, which beats 100,000 times a day to transport oxygen and vital nutrients to every cell in the body, yet we do so little to keep it healthy. Coronary health and diet are closely linked so the good news is that there is much you can do to reduce the chances of heart disease.

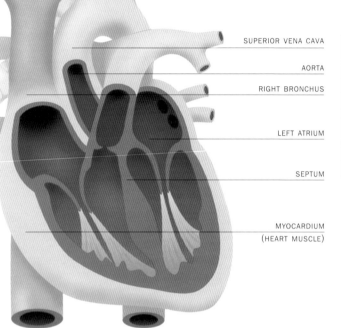

SUPERIOR VENA CAVA

AORTA

RIGHT BRONCHUS

LEFT ATRIUM

SEPTUM

MYOCARDIUM
(HEART MUSCLE)

The heart is a miracle of engineering that pumps blood first to the lungs to be oxygenated and then out via the aorta around the body to individual cells. Heart disease is now responsible for more deaths in the US and UK than any other illness, and puts a great strain on hospitals and emergency services (above right).

The big breakthrough that nutritionists believe will improve our cardiovascular health and save more lives than any other is the discovery in the blood of a compound called homocysteine. This substance, which is formed during protein metabolism when the amino acid methionine is converted to cysteine, is 40 times a more accurate predictor of heart disease and stroke than cholesterol. Raised levels of homocysteine have been found in the blood of up to 40 percent of patients suffering from heart disease, for example.

Astonishingly, the discovery is not new: the Harvard scientist who first discovered the importance of homocysteine first published his results 30 years ago.

Homocysteine is believed to damage the arteries by interfering with the blood vessels and causing the build-up of dangerous plaque deposits in the coronary arteries—a condition known as atherosclerosis in which the arteries thicken and harden. Angina, an excruciating pain in the chest,

is often the first outward sign of a heart problem and is almost always due to atherosclerosis, indicating that blood flow has become restricted because the blood vessels have narrowed. High blood pressure is also a symptom of atherosclerosis: it occurs because the heart has to pump harder to get blood through narrowed arteries.

Fortunately, you can use diet and supplementation to help lower homocysteine levels and prevent atherosclerosis. You should follow a diet based on wholegrains and antioxidant fruit and vegetables and reduce your intake of saturated fat (found principally in animal products). Vegetarians tend to have lower blood pressure and lower rates of heart disease and stroke than meateaters. Although meat is an abundant source of iron, which is needed to make healthy red blood cells, there are plenty of good vegetable sources of this nutrient.

Raised levels of homocysteine are found in people who are deficient in folic acid, and vitamins B_6 and B_{12}. Research shows that taking daily supplements of these nutrients can reduce levels.

The antioxidant nutrients—selenium and vitamins A, C, and E—are also important in protecting against heart disease. Vitamin E is believed to be the most important of these, in fact several studies have shown that vitamin E levels in the blood are, again, a more accurate indicator of risk of heart disease than cholesterol levels.

Foods for a Healthy Heart

To lower homocysteine levels eat foods that are rich in folic acid and vitamins B_6 and B_{12}. Good sources include:

Folic acid—spinach, asparagus, Brussels sprouts, lima beans, soybeans, organic organ meats, brewers' yeast, root vegetables, whole-grains, wheat germ, kidney beans, bulgur wheat, oysters, salmon, orange juice, avocados, and organic milk.

Vitamin B_6—avocados, bananas, carrots, lentils, brown rice, bran, soybeans, sunflower seeds, tuna, salmon, wheat germ, and whole-wheat flour.

Vitamin B_{12}—organic beef, cheese, eggs, fish, clams, organic milk, and dairy products.

For general protection against the risk of stroke and heart disease eat fewer fatty and processed foods and more foods rich in the following:

Antioxidants—yams, butternut and winter squash, pumpkin, carrots, spinach, broccoli, iceberg lettuce, endive, kale, tomatoes, melon, apricots, mango, and papaya.

Selenium—tuna, herring, oysters, clams, sesame seeds, Brazil nuts, sunflower seeds, wholegrains, and brewers' yeast.

Magnesium—seafood, wholegrains, dark green vegetables, molasses, and nuts.

Potassium—lean meats, red snapper, salmon, yogurt, wholegrains, potatoes, avocados, bananas, apricots, melon, tomato juice, orange juice, peaches, prunes, soybeans, lima beans, Swiss chard, yams, spinach, dried fruits, and sunflower seeds.

Iron—eggs, fish, poultry, cherry juice, green leafy vegetables, dried fruits, liver, meat, and organ meats.

Magnesium and potassium are both essential for cardiovascular health. Magnesium is readily available in lots of foods, but many people are deficient because they eat a diet high in meat and dairy products as well as processed and refined foods, which have had the magnesium stripped out.

A low potassium and high sodium (salt) diet is linked to high blood pressure. Dietary potassium will lower blood pressure and has been found to be particularly useful in treating people over the age of 65, who often do not respond well to the drugs commonly used to lower blood pressure.

A diet rich in fish, seafood, legumes, fruit, and vegetables will keep your heart in top condition.

Energy
Boosters

Can you recall that post-vacation feeling when you were brimming with health and boundless energy? To recreate it all the year round, you need to eat a good diet and get plenty of regular exercise. Research reveals that nutritional deficiencies and food intolerances can deplete energy levels more than was once realized, and that they also contribute to the debilitating condition, Chronic Fatigue Syndrome, which has become so prevalent in the West.

If you identify more with the tired person on the right rather than with the healthy person on the left, your diet may be lacking vital nutrients.

It is important to eat a healthy diet because a deficiency in any nutrient can cause fatigue and make the body more susceptible to infection.

If you have been suffering from a debilitating exhaustion for six months or more and if no other underlying cause has been found, you could have what is now known as Chronic Fatigue Syndrome (CFS).

This condition was only officially named and defined by the United States Center for Diseases Control (CDC) in 1988. In fact, it is anything but new. Still a controversial medical diagnosis, it has been known about since the 1860s, and has flourished under a number of different names. In the UK, for example, it is still called Myalgic Encephalomyelitis (ME). In the credit-mad, spend, spend, spend 1980s it was known as Yuppie Flu. Some people call it Postviral Fatigue Syndrome and others Post-Infectious Neuromyasthenia.

Whatever the name, the symptoms, which come and go, are likely to include a mild fever, a recurrent sore throat, swollen lymph nodes, weak muscles, a recurrent headache, depression, insomnia or an excessive need for sleep, joint pain, and prolonged fatigue after any form of exercise.

The reason CFS remains controversial is because scientists still cannot agree on a single cause—there are several theories—and many doctors still believe it to be entirely psychosomatic.

The very latest thinking is that it could be caused by an innate abnormality in regulating blood pressure followed by a viral infection that leaves lasting damage to the immune system. The blood pressure theory came into being following the results of an American study that found that at the point when the heart needs to speed up to deal with exertion, in CFS sufferers it actually slows down. This abnormality cannot be detected by normal tests for blood pressure, but in one study it was present in 22 out of 23 CFS patients. The researchers speculated that a subsequent viral infection then triggered CFS.

The viruses incriminated but still not proven guilty include Epstein-Barr, the human *Herpes simplex*, and the Coxsackie B organisms. Orthodox medicine has concentrated its efforts on searching for a viral cause for the condition, while complementary medicine practitioners take steps to reduce susceptibility and to support the immune system of patients so they can deal more effectively with an invading organism.

Both fibromyalgia (FM) and Multiple Chemical Sensitivity (MCS) produce symptoms that are similar to those of Chronic Fatigue Syndrome and the exact diagnosis of your condition will depend on the bias of the doctor you see. In addition, many pre-existing conditions and their treatments can also cause chronic fatigue. Depression has also been found to be the most common cause and CFS has long been recognized as a key feature in food allergies, which have been diagnosed in up to 85 percent of CFS sufferers.

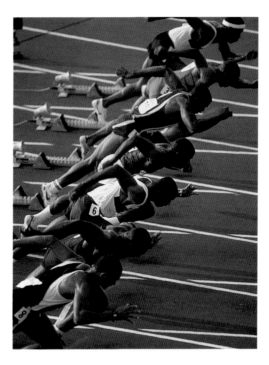

Coenzyme Q10 is taken by athletes to boost energy and stamina.

HOW TO BOOST ENERGY LEVELS

Low blood-sugar levels can cause depression, low energy levels, and chronic fatigue. Sufferers should cut down on sugar and refined carbohydrates, cut out coffee, and step up their intake of energy-giving protein.

One of the most exciting discoveries in the treatment of chronic fatigue is a powerful antioxidant called Coenzyme Q10 (CoQ10), a vitaminlike substance said to act in the body in a similar way to vitamin E.

Oily fish, nuts, and spinach should make a regular appearance in everyone's diet, because they contain Coenzyme Q10 to boost energy.

Energy **Boosters**

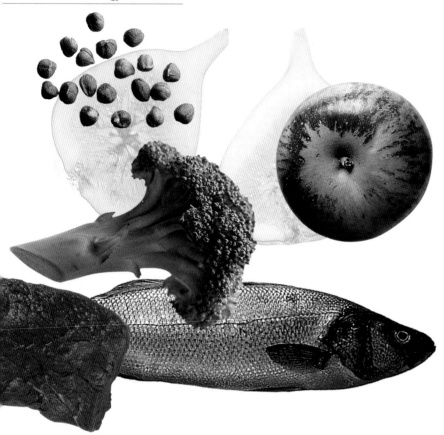

If you lack energy, eat plenty of fish, green leafy vegetables, fruit, and lean meat, which are all good sources of magnesium.

A coenzyme works alongside an enzyme. An enzyme is a protein that acts as a catalyst to bring about chemical changes. Coenzyme Q10 is needed by every single cell in the body to produce energy and is often taken by athletes to increase stamina and endurance. It boosts circulation, increasing the amount of oxygen received by the tissues. It also increases energy levels, has powerful antiaging properties, and is believed to help strengthen muscles.

Coenzyme Q10 also bolsters the immune system and has been shown to counter histamine (a substance that is produced in an allergic reaction), which helps it to prevent the allergies that can often cause CFS. Coenzyme Q10 has also been used to treat mental disorders, including depression, another cause of CFS.

Coenzyme Q10 may be taken as a supplement, but good food sources include spinach, tuna, sardines, peanuts, mackerel, sesame, legumes, and bran. It is easily destroyed by cooking, storing, and processing but marinated sardines (*see page 46*) are an excellent source because no cooking is involved.

BENEFICIAL MAGNESIUM

Magnesium is crucial to the activity of the enzymes and coenzymes involved in the production of energy. Even a slight deficiency in this important mineral can cause chronic fatigue and CFS-type symptoms. A blood sample will give an accurate picture of the body's magnesium levels. Most CFS patients, tested this way, have lower magnesium levels than nonsufferers.

Magnesium is known as the antistress mineral. It boosts the uptake of both calcium and potassium, a deficiency of which interferes with the transmission of nerve and muscle impulses, causing irritability and nervousness.

Most foods contain some magnesium, but particularly rich sources include fish, meat, seafood, dairy products, green leafy vegetables, wholegrains, nuts, lemons, figs, apples, apricots, bananas, and brown rice. Avoid heavy drinking, which lowers magnesium levels. If you are going to take a supplement, buy a product in which the magnesium is bound to either aspartate or citrate, both of which help fight fatigue.

Dandelions are rich in vitamin C for energy. Use the leaves in salads and make the petals into wine.

Take up a form of exercise that you enjoy, such as dancing, to boost your energy levels.

VITAMIN C FOR ENERGY

Most animals can make their own vitamin C, but people, apes, and guinea pigs must glean theirs from their diet. This valuable substance is a powerful immune enhancer and is essential for tissue growth and repair. It also boosts the absorption of iron, which is critical for both energy production and a healthy immune system.

High doses of vitamin C have been given to CFS patients with good results. For chronic fatigue, a daily dose of 3000mg (1g x 3 a day) is recommended. Good food sources include broccoli, asparagus, dandelion greens (*see Dandelion and Pancetta Salad page 52*), citrus fruits, sweet peppers, green peas, spinach, strawberries, Swiss chard, watercress, pineapple, kale, lemons, Kiwifruit, cabbage, cauliflower, and mangoes. Avoid smoking, which seriously depletes vitamin C stores.

HEALING HERBS

Herbal remedies for CFS include Siberian ginseng which, as well as supporting adrenal function, helps increase resistance to stress by boosting the number of T-cells and Natural Killer Cells which fight off disease. Licorice root, which has strong antiviral properties, will also support the immune system, but only take with an herbalist's advice since it may raise blood pressure in strong doses.

ENERGY-BOOSTING EXERCISE

If you don't suffer from CFS but you do feel tired all the time, you need to take up some form of moderate exercise, which boosts energy levels by releasing endorphins which, in turn, help banish depression. You don't have to start training for the New York or London marathon: 30 minutes of modest exercise, three times a week with a rest day in between will do more than anything else to increase both your stamina and vitality.

"Mushroom" tea

The Kombucha or Manchurian "mushroom" is not a mushroom at all, but a large, flat, pancake-shaped funguslike growth that is a combination of health-promoting lichen and beneficial bacteria. It has long been used in Asia as a natural energy booster and is fast gaining credence among CFS sufferers worldwide. A potent detoxifier and immune enhancer, it has been said to slow and even reverse the aging process, help fight diseases including CFS, cancer, Multiple Sclerosis (MS), and AIDS. It is not eaten, but turned into a strong antiviral and antibacterial tea by leaving it to ferment for 7–10 days in a mixture of water, sugar, green or black tea, and cider vinegar. Russian researchers have found the tea's antibiotic activity is at its peak after 7– 8 days and kept this way, your mix will produce "daughter" mushrooms, which can then be used to make more tea. There are now 10 million Kombucha tea drinkers worldwide.

Emotional Health

Job insecurity, money worries, relationship problems, increasing fragmentation of family life—there are many reasons why we all get depressed from time to time. However, in some people depression is persistent and has no obvious external cause. Many ordinary foods have extraordinary powers and, if you are prone to dark moods, you should consider changing your diet to include foods that promote well-being.

Depression is the most common emotional disorder and it affects a large proportion of the population: 30 million Americans take antidepressants every year. It can be the result of an underlying disorder such as food allergies, or Chronic Fatigue Syndrome (*see page 174*), and it can also be a side effect of prescription drugs, including the contraceptive pill, anti-inflammatories, tranquilizers, and sedatives. Stress is a common cause of depression: researchers now believe we are biologically programmed to react to extreme stress by becoming depressed.

The symptoms typically include disturbed sleep patterns and insomnia, which then set up a cycle of fatigue and depression; digestive disorders, tiredness, headaches, and forgetfulness; muscle pain, weight loss or weight gain; and a withdrawal from both work and home life. People who are suffering from depression will no longer take pleasure in the things they used to enjoy. Instead, they feel that they have no control over their lives.

For severe cases of depression, antidepressants can make the difference between life and death (in clinical depression, recurrent thoughts of suicide are common), but they are not recommended for those suffering less severe forms since the side effects include a dry mouth, abnormal heart rate, bloating, confusion, impotence, and loss of libido.

Foods for Well-Being

Tryptophan is an amino acid that is needed for the production of vitamin B_3 (niacin) and for the manufacture of serotonin, the body's own "feel-good" substance. Tryptophan supplements are still banned in the US after a link between a blood

*St. John's wort—
the sunshine herb.*

disorder and supplements containing the amino acid was found. (Subsequent research suggested the problem was due to other contaminants in these products.) The best dietary sources of tryptophan include brown rice, cottage cheese, meat, peanuts, baked potatoes with their skin, roasted pumpkin, dried sunflower seeds, seaweed, milk, turnip greens, and soy.

To convert tryptophan in the body to niacin you need sufficient levels of vitamin B_6 (pyridoxine). Foods that are excellent sources of vitamin B_6 include avocados, bananas, carrots, lentils, brown rice, bran, soybeans, sunflower seeds, tuna, salmon, and whole-wheat flour.

All the B vitamins can help fight depression because they help relieve stress, but the most important—folic acid—is the one in which most people are deficient. Natural sources include spinach, asparagus, root vegetables, soybeans, organ meats, wholegrains, bulghur wheat, kidney beans, oysters, orange juice, and avocados.

To combat depression, take 800mcg a day, with a vitamin B_{12} supplement because these work together. Folic acid deficiency can mask a deficiency of vitamin B_{12} which is common (especially in the over-60s), and can cause confusion, memory loss, and apathy. As well as vitamin B foods, fatty acids in fish can help lift mood as they are believed to play a crucial role in brain chemistry, so eat more salmon, halibut, sea bass, and sardines.

MINERALS, VITAMINS, AND HERBS

Magnesium, found in most foods, but especially in figs, lemons, almonds, nuts, seeds, apples, and dark green vegetables, also helps ease depression by relieving stress. Vitamin C, with its antiallergy and antistress properties, can help for the same reasons, and for people with moderate depression, selenium, which is found in seafood, has been shown to elevate mood.

Described as nature's Prozac, St. John's wort is an excellent antidepressant that is very successful in treating mild to moderate depression without causing side effects. For anxiety, insomnia, and restlessness, the herbal remedy Kava kava (*see page 183*) has a very soothing effect helping to promote a feeling of calm and well-being.

5-HTP

A chemical that brings us one step closer to the manufacture of the mood chemical, serotonin, is 5-Hydroxytryptophan (5-HTP), which is available in supplement form and is said to be safer than tryptophan supplements because it is extracted from the seed of an African plant (*Griffonia simplicifolia*). It has been shown to be as effective as and even better than the standard anti-depressant drugs and has none of the unpleasant side effects. 5-HTP also improves the quality of sleep and increases the release of endorphins which help fight depression.

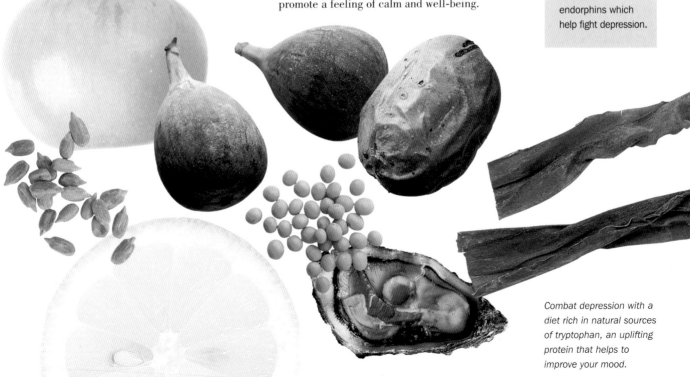

Combat depression with a diet rich in natural sources of tryptophan, an uplifting protein that helps to improve your mood.

Defeating
Cancer

The word cancer comes from the Greek karkinos, meaning crab, referring to the disease's uneven, sideways progress through the body. The biggest killer after coronary artery disease, cancer is understandably feared. However, research studies have shown conclusively that changing your diet and lifestyle can dramatically reduce your risk of contracting the disease.

To reduce your risk of cancer, avoid industrial pollutants and cigarette smoke, which are both carcinogenic, and only consume alcohol and fatty foods in moderation.

Cancer experts estimate that soon after the beginning of the 21st century, between 40 and 50 percent of the population will develop some form of cancer during their lives. Yet despite increasingly sophisticated medical intervention, we are still no closer to curing this dreaded disease.

According to the US National Cancer Institute, 50 percent of all cancers may be preventable through diet and lifestyle changes. This is because colon and rectal cancers, for example, which have reached virtually epidemic levels in the West, are almost unheard of in the East. Only a small percentage of cases of both cancers are caused by a genetic flaw, meaning that the real culprit must be the high-fat, low-fiber diet that is typical in the West. Happily, this means that making changes to your lifestyle and diet can dramatically reduce your risk of cancer. It is in the prevention of cancer that the idea of food as medicine really comes into its own. In his book

The Cancer Prevention Diet, Michio Kushi, an expert on macrobiotic eating and a pioneer of the natural foods movement, states, "The proper place to perform cancer surgery is not in the operating room, after the disease has run its course, but in the kitchen and in other areas of daily life before it has developed.

"By removing certain foods from the pantry and the refrigerator, replacing them with the proper quality and variety of foods, and applying proper cooking methods together with correcting environmental conditions and our daily way of life, we can ensure that cancers and other degenerative diseases do not arise."

Of course this idea is not new: it was Hippocrates, the father of modern medicine, who said, "Let food be thy medicine." He was also the first person to identify cancer some 2,500 years ago in ancient Greece and coined the word *karkinos*, from which our word cancer comes.

BENEFICIAL FOODS

A healthy diet and lifestyle is the cornerstone of your fight against cancer. You should eat less saturated fat, fewer processed foods, and increase your intake of wholegrains and fruit and vegetables.

There are many books devoted solely to cancer and diet and here I just want to highlight the three most potent weapons in your armory—antioxidants, phytochemicals, and calcium.

Antioxidants are important because they both mop up and prevent the formation of free radicals, which are unstable oxygen atoms that, if left unchecked, bind with other atoms and produce a form of energy that can damage healthy cells, causing them to mutate. This process sets off the chain of events that can lead to cancer. Environmental factors that promote the formation of damaging free radicals include tobacco smoke, air pollutants, pesticides, and solvents.

The most potent antioxidants are the vitamins A, C, and E. The trace minerals selenium and zinc have also shown excellent anticancer properties. To consume enough antioxidants to protect yourself from cancer, you need to eat at least 3–5 servings of fresh fruit and vegetables every day. Because very few people achieve this target, you may want to consider antioxidant supplements.

Phytochemicals, substances that occur naturally in plant foods (*see page 26*), are now believed to reduce cancer risk. They are thought responsible for keeping the number of deaths from cancer in the East much lower than in the West. You are 20 times more likely to die from breast or prostate cancer than people living in Asian cultures who eat a diet rich in phytochemical foods such as soy.

Estrogen is believed to encourage damaged cells, which can lie dormant for years, to start dividing, developing eventually into cancer. Phytochemicals are thought to supplant harmful estrogen causing it to be flushed out of the body. Not only can phytochemicals help prevent cancer, some

Citrus fruit, vegetables, and soybeans contain phytochemicals, beneficial compounds that protect the body from cancer.

researchers believe they can reverse the changes that cause cancer in the first place, turning mutated cells back into healthy ones.

The most powerful phytoestrogen-rich food is soy. Eat at least one soy product a day, but avoid products that have been genetically modified.

Lots of people supplement their calcium intake to build and maintain healthy teeth and bones, but few realize the mineral may also protect against cancers of the colon and rectum, which are now the third biggest cancer killers in the UK and the second in the US. In one US study of 25,000 people, those who took 1200mg of calcium daily had a 50 percent reduced risk of colon cancer.

What is Cancer?

Every minute, some 10 million cells in your body are in the process of dividing. Healthy cells know just when to do this and when to stop, but cancer cells lose this ability. Somewhere between one in a million and one in 100 million cell divisions, something goes wrong and a cancer cell is the result. The cells proliferate rapidly and produce a ball of cancer cells that disrupt the healthy tissues around them. The mass of abnormal cells continues to grow to become a tumor which, if untreated, will interfere with the functioning of nearby organs and, eventually, cause death. Two common types of cancer are breast cancer (above left) and lung cancer (above right).

Avoiding **Stress**

Too much stress is to blame for many disorders ranging from insomnia and depression to high blood pressure. If you suffer frequently from stress-related ailments, you need to take a long look at your lifestyle. In particular you should make time for yourself. It may seem indulgent to spend time unwinding with the newspapers but "me time" is an important investment in your own health. So, too, is eating plenty of foods rich in stress-busting B vitamins and minerals such as magnesium and calcium.

Highway drivers have to be in a constant state of alert watching out for dangers, and stress levels soar as a result.

Events most likely to trigger a stress reaction are job pressures, family arguments, financial worries, and deadlines. It is now believed that stress is a factor in 80 percent of illnesses and accounts for more than two-thirds of visits to the family doctor. The symptoms may include high blood pressure, back and neck pain, dizziness, diarrhea, insomnia, fatigue, tearfulness, poor concentration, sexual dysfunction, loss of appetite, or overeating.

A modest amount of stress from time to time may sharpen your performance at work or help you pass an exam, but constant stress will eventually kill you. In animal studies, prolonged stress has been shown to kill perfectly healthy heart cells, damage the immune system, raise blood-sugar levels, and even cause the bones to thin, increasing the risk of osteoporosis. It is also known that stress increases the number of harmful free radicals in the body.

GENERAL ADAPTATION SYNDROME

Stress upsets the body's equilibrium causing a number of biological changes known collectively as the General Adaptation Syndrome (GAS).

There are three distinct phases to GAS. During the initial, alarm stage, you spend your time worrying that you cannot do everything you know you must do. This phase is short-lived and is caused by the flight-or-fight response our ancestors relied on for survival. You then enter the more prolonged and damaging resistance phase, in which you don't want to do everything you know you must do, and have to push yourself harder to achieve less. During this phase, your blood pressure increases to help you cope with all the demands on you. You may feel you have more energy, but in reality you are running on empty and there is a long-term price to pay—exhaustion—the final stage. When you reach this stage you are well on the road toward a major illness.

All three GAS stages affect the adrenal glands, which regulate hormone levels and can become worn out and exhausted when we place too many unrelenting pressures on ourselves. Recurrent infections and illness, which are the result of an impaired immune system, can also be a sign of stress.

Beat stress the natural way with a diet rich in seafood, oily fish, nuts and fruit and vegetables.

MANAGING STRESS

Changing your diet is probably one of the most effective ways to manage stress. The B vitamins are known as nature's own antidote to stress. They work best together, so as well as eating foods that supply the various B-type vitamins, take a good B-complex combination supplement.

The body uses up vitamin C more quickly than usual during stressful periods. If pressure is prolonged, the tissues could become depleted of this crucial vitamin. You can avoid deficiency by drinking the juice of vitamin C-rich fruits and vegetables, especially Kiwifruit, which are even richer in vitamin C than the oranges that sailors were once given to stop them from getting scurvy.

Both calcium and magnesium also play a crucial role in beating stress by helping to lower blood pressure, which rises when you are under pressure. If you're avoiding dairy products, natural sources of calcium include broccoli, tofu, soybeans, okra, shellfish, mackerel, salmon, and sardines. Good natural sources of magnesium include seafood, wholegrains, dark green leafy vegetables, and nuts.

LIFESTYLE AND HERBAL REMEDIES

The stress hormones prepare the body for action (called the "fight or flight" response) and the very best way to minimize their negative effects is to burn them off with regular exercise. Try walking or swimming three times a week.

Exercise also releases endorphins, which can help to improve mood. If you are feeling stressed, avoid all stimulants, especially coffee, alcohol, and cigarettes. You may think that these substances will help to calm you down, but in fact they do the opposite.

Kava kava, the Pacific Island herb first discovered by Captain Cook, helps to promote a feeling of calm and well-being, especially in times of severe stress and anxiety. A natural tranquilizer, Kava kava can help break the vicious cycle of stress-induced insomnia that is caused by anxiety about poor performance, which in turn generates more stress.

DHEA

As we age, it takes our bodies longer to recover from stress. We also have lower levels of a hormone called dehydroepiandro-styerone (DHEA), which researchers now believe can help counter the effects of stress. DHEA is produced by the adrenal glands, which sit on top of the kidneys. It is the most abundant hormone found in the bloodstream and is also thought to have an antiaging effect, slowing down the production of fats, hormones, and acids. At 40, you have half the amount of DHEA you had at 20, which is unfortunate because animal studies have shown this hormone can counter the damaging physical effects of prolonged stress by restoring levels of the stress hormones back to normal. Most DHEA supplements you buy have been extracted from wild yams,

Wild yams are a natural source of DHEA.

which contain substances the body can then convert into DHEA. High doses may suppress your body's ability to make DHEA at all and if you do take a supplement, you should take it alongside a good antioxidant to prevent any damage to the liver. DHEA can be bought over the counter in the United States but is only available on prescription in the United Kingdom.

Brisk walking in the fresh air dissipates the effect of stress hormones and stimulates the release of endorphins—the body's "feel-good" hormones.

Hormones and Health

The evidence of large-scale hormonal disruption is compelling: worldwide studies suggest sperm counts have dropped by half in the last 50 years. One in seven couples experience infertility, and breast cancer has almost tripled in the last 30 years. Environmental pollutants and use of synthetic hormones for contraception, fertility, and menopause management are playing havoc with our hormonal systems. To safeguard your health, avoid pollutants and eat protective foods.

HYPOTHALAMUS   PITUITARY GLAND

THYROID

LIVER

ADRENAL GLAND   KIDNEY

UTERUS

OVARY

TESTES

Scientists investigating conditions linked to disturbed hormones blame the increased and widespread use of chemicals in the environment, food production, and pharmaceutical treatments. They believe these chemicals disrupt the delicate balance of the body's hormones.

Hormones serve as the body's messengers. Secreted directly into the bloodstream by different organs, each has a specific job. Collectively, the hormone-producing organs are known as the endocrine system. Its major organs are the hypothalamus, the pituitary gland, the thyroid gland, the parathyroid glands, the islets of the pancreas, the adrenal glands, the testes, and the ovaries. In pregnancy, the placenta also acts as an endocrine gland.

The hypothalamus secretes hormones that stimulate the pituitary gland. Some trigger the release of pituitary hormones, for example, while others suppress them. The pituitary gland is seen as the master gland because it co-ordinates much of the endocrine system, but not all the other

The endocrine system (left) secretes hormones, chemical substances that orchestrate every bodily function including the production of sperm (right).

hormone-producing glands are under its control. Some respond instead to concentrations of certain substances in the blood. The insulin-secreting pancreas, for example, responds to glucose and fatty acids; the parathyroid cells respond to calcium and phosphate.

Most hormones are proteins. Some are steroids, which are fatty substances derived from cholesterol. Both types of hormone work by binding to specific receptors either on the surface of or inside the cell. Once in place, they can change the cell's functioning. They control your growth and development, reproduction, and sexual characteristics. They influence the way the body uses and stores energy. They control the volume of fluid and the levels of salt and sugar in the blood. In short, they control everything.

THREATS TO HORMONE BALANCE

Many chemicals, including lots of pesticides, mimic the role of estrogen in our bodies and stimulate the growth of hormone-sensitive tissue. The effect is to disrupt hormones and confuse the messages they are sending out.

As well has eating fruit and vegetables with pesticide-traces, we also take in estrogen from meat and dairy products. Animals are frequently

fed a high-protein diet and pumped full of hormones to force rapid growth for more profit. Both meat and dairy products can also act as a storehouse for non-biodegradable toxins that we know disrupt hormone levels.

Lifestyle factors also upset the hormonal balance. Prolonged stress, for instance, produces too much epinephrine and cortisol. Any stimulant, including coffee and cigarettes, results in the body producing cortisol, which increases the production of estrogen and competes with progesterone for receptor sites, further upsetting the fragile balance of these two important hormones. The long-term consequences of a permanent state of stress can be impaired liver function and an inability to flush toxins from the system.

PROTECT YOUR HEALTH

Your first, most important step is to avoid the chemicals that you know can disrupt hormones. To avoid pesticides and herbicides, for example, always try to buy organic produce. Alternatively, even grow some of your own fruit and vegetables, without the use of chemicals. If you cannot obtain organic foods, always wash and peel fruit and vegetables before you eat them.

Cut back on both meat and dairy foods, which we know can contain hormones, and when you do eat meat, try to buy it from an organic supplier. The non-biodegradable toxins that disrupt hormones accumulate in animal fat, so cutting back on meat and dairy foods will help reduce your risk of a hormone-related condition.

Chemicals used in packaging can seep into the food itself. Reduce this risk by never heating food in plastic containers and by minimizing the contact between plastic and the food you plan to eat. For example, pack and take your vegetables home in paper bags.

The digestive tract produces lots of hormones that work with the nervous system to maintain healthy digestion and absorption. Nutritionists now believe that many of the symptoms usually attributed to hormonal imbalances—including weight gain, water retention, bloating, anxiety, and depression—are more likely to be caused

by an undetected digestive problem (*see page 160*). Even those who do have a true hormonal problem will improve more rapidly when the digestion is in optimum health.

It makes sense to investigate natural alternatives to HRT for managing the symptoms of menopause and to use other forms of contraception instead of the pill. Women approaching menopause might try eating plenty of soy, citrus fruits, vegetables, cereals, onion, garlic, broccoli, cabbage, and cauliflower. These foods contain substances known as phytoestrogens (*see page 26*), which have a natural estrogenic effect in the body.

Combat PMS the natural way with foods brimming in vitamin B_6 such as soy and avocados.

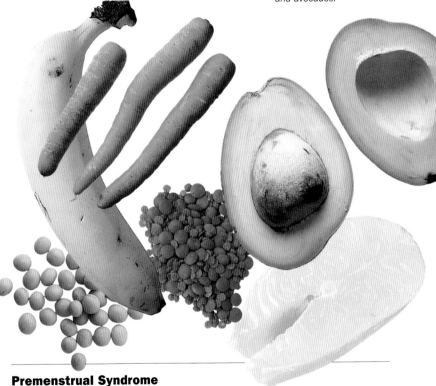

Premenstrual Syndrome

Some 75 percent of women suffer from premenstrual syndrome (PMS). With the tendency for puberty to start earlier and earlier—the average age is 11 today compared with 17 in the nineteenth century—PMS will affect women for longer. The symptoms vary between women, but the more common ones include anxiety, irritability, mood swings, fluid retention, breast tenderness, weight gain, acne, fatigue, and a craving for sweet foods. Most sufferers have high levels of estrogen and low levels of progesterone. To reduce excess estrogen, cut back on meat and dairy products and eat foods that are rich in vitamin B_6. These include avocados, bananas, carrots, lentils, brown rice, bran, soybeans, sunflower seeds, tuna, salmon, and whole-wheat flour. In tests, a daily B_6 supplement of up to 800mcg has been shown to reduce estrogen and boost progesterone levels.

Healthy **Kids**

Restaurant "kids' menus" often typify what many people regard as suitable food for children: french fries, chicken nuggets, hamburgers, ketchup, and desserts—with not a green vegetable in sight. This is a terrible state of affairs since eating well in childhood is crucial for laying the foundations of good health. A healthy diet that is child-friendly need not be a contradiction in terms, and by taking the trouble to prepare wholesome meals you will be setting your child up for a long and healthy life.

A healthy, nutritious diet based on wholegrains, fresh fruit, vegetables, legumes, and moderate quantities of lean, organically-produced meat and fish will give your children all the energy and strength they need. It will also increase their resistance to illness. Unfortunately, this is not the kind of diet that most children receive.

In the US, childhood obesity has increased by 54 percent since 1976. A number of trends have contributed to this. Children get less exercise— many no longer walk to school, for example. Also, eating habits have changed during the last few decades. Many families no longer eat a home-cooked meal together preferring to graze on microwaved, high-fat ready meals. Youngsters who spend all their leisure time glued to the television or the computer and who eat high-fat, low-fiber diets are at risk of developing the same high cholesterol levels as their couch-potato parents. Worse, researchers suspect the unthinkable: that because of their high-fat diet, many children may already be in the early stages of heart disease with arteries that are already narrowed.

BRAND LOYALTY

Children develop brand loyalty from an early age. When they are watching television aimed at children, they are also being bombarded by junk food commercials. These frequently use cartoon characters to make the product more appealing since, for a young child, there is no distinction between a favorite program and a clever ad.

To give your child boundless energy, feed her a nutritious diet that contains plenty of fresh fruit and vegetables.

In the US, children spend $2 billion a year on food products and influence the spending of another $75 billion. You can see why manufacturers will spend whatever it takes to catch children as young as they can.

PESTICIDES

Proportionally for their size, children eat more fruit and vegetables than adults do—a child of preschool age eats the equivalent of around six times more fresh fruit than his or her parents—which should, of course, mean they are healthier. If it wasn't for the widespread use of pesticides and herbicides, they probably would be. However, the use of chemicals by food growers has increased ten-fold in the last half century and children are most at risk from the effects.

The US Environmental Protection Agency (EPA), has identified 66 different carcinogenic pesticides that turn up in the average child's diet. And that's just the ones they can find. Current testing techniques can only identify 40 percent of possible chemical contaminants and it cannot detect any of the metabolites, which can form when the component chemicals break down in the body and which pose an even greater threat to your family's health than the chemicals themselves.

HOW TO HELP YOUR KIDS

Children copy and learn from their parents. They will eat what you eat, which means that you can lay the foundations of good health in their lives by making healthy choices for the whole family. If you think that sounds difficult, you are absolutely right, because your children will want to eat exactly the same diet as their friends.

To encourage brand loyalty, manufacturers deliberately produce snacks and candies in appealing shapes.

Healthy **Kids**

Use honey as a healthier alternative to sugar for sweetening children's yogurt and other foods.

Many children go through a "fussy" stage and parents worry that they are not getting sufficient nutrients. However, as long as they eat foods from all the different food groups, there should be no cause for concern.

Children need three meals a day, plus wholesome snacks and plenty of pure water. Always serve one vegetable and one grain dish with each meal; for menu suggestions see pages 132–143. Both breakfast and lunch should be larger meals than supper. Preschool children do not have the same capacity as older ones and may prefer to eat little and often, so keep plenty of nutritious snacks on hand, such as yogurt, raisins, cheese cubes, and breadsticks.

Your hardest job is to reduce the amount of sugar your child eats. Try to save chocolate, candy, and refined products such as cookies, cakes, and potato chips for occasional treats and when cooking for kids, use sugar substitutes such as honey or rice syrup. Offer fresh fruit or yogurt

Fast food need not be unhealthy. Make pizza for your children with low-fat cheese piled high with delicious vegetables, then finish with a glass of milk.

Scrub all fruit and vegetables thoroughly to remove the skin that may contain traces of harmful herbicides.

as dessert instead of sugar-laden puddings. On the other hand, don't let teenagers, especially girls, get hung up about their weight since eating disorders that start in childhood can wreck adult lives. In fact, dump the bathroom scales and explain that eating a healthy diet will help keep them slim. It is better to monitor weight gain by keeping an eye on how clothes fit rather than obsessively counting calories.

More than anything else, eating should be a pleasure. Make mealtimes fun for your child by introducing new exciting dishes and serving food in a fun way. For example, decorating a pizza with a couple of olives and a slice of pepper to make a face (*see pages 132–3*) will tempt even the most reluctant eater.

FOOD SAFETY

Only one percent of the produce in your supermarket has been tested for pesticides, so if you cannot buy organic produce that has been grown without chemicals, make sure you wash everything thoroughly. Using a mixture of warm

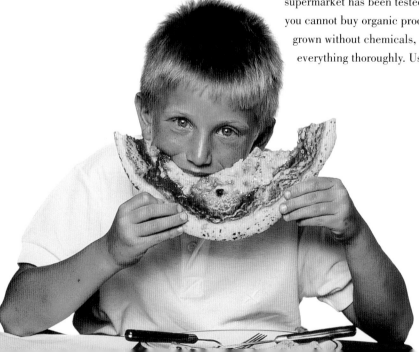

water and vinegar speeds up the breakdown of many pesticides. Always remove the outer leaves of vegetables such as lettuce and cabbage, because these often have a higher concentration of chemicals than the inner leaves. Scrub and peel all root vegetables, including carrots, turnips, and potatoes. Scrub and peel any fruits that have been waxed to make them shiny.

Install a water purification system so your family can drink plenty of pure water and make your own fruit juices to avoid the risk of contaminants seeping into the juice from the plastic lining of the carton.

VITAMINS AND MINERALS

Some vitamins, including vitamin C and all the B vitamins are water-soluble. This means that if they are not absorbed by the body that day they are excreted. Your child needs these vitamins every day and you should take this into account

Avoiding Obesity

Childhood obesity is not only a major problem in the West, but is also a growing problem in countries that have abandoned their traditional, healthy diet in favor of the high-fat, low-fiber, highly processed diet that is to blame for the increase in so many degenerative diseases. To keep your child's weight at an optimum and healthy level, always check the fat content of any food they eat. It is suggested that no more than 30 percent of a child's total daily calories should come from fat. Each gram of fat is the equivalent of 9 calories. So if, for example, 2 tablespoons of peanut butter contains 15g of fat and 200 calories, you can work out that 15 x 9 = 135. This means that 135 of the 200 calories come from fat. Do this calculation for every meal (read all the labels) and if the calories from fat add up to more than 30 percent of the total calorie intake, make a determined effort to cut back on the amount of fat your child is eating.

If getting your child to eat fruit is a struggle, serve a fruit smoothie instead. Liquidize half a banana with 3 strawberries and a little apple juice and serve in a tall glass with a novelty straw.

when planning meals. Fat-soluble vitamins, which include vitamins A, D, E, and K, remain stable at low cooking temperatures, but they are depleted by antibiotics and other prescription drugs.

If you feed children a balanced organic diet, you should not need to give them mineral and vitamin supplements, except when they are unwell or run down. When choosing a brand, avoid those that are targeted at children, which may be sweetened with sugar or artificial sweeteners to make them more appealing. Instead find a formulation that is sweetened with honey or rice syrup. Always give your child supplements with food and if they do have to take antibiotics, help repopulate the good bacteria that keep the gut healthy by feeding them live natural yogurt—try the recipe for Homemade Bulgarian-Style Yogurt on page 132.

Index A–Z

Useful
addresses

National Institute of Nutrition
265 Carling Avenue, Suite 302
Ottawa, Ontario
Canada K1S 2E1
Tel: 613 235 3355

Health Service Centre
971 Bloor Street West
Toronto, Ontario
Canada
Tel: 905 535 9562
Natural foods, supplements, books, herbal remedies.
Various locations, mail order

GNC-General Nutrition Centre
6299 Airport Road, Suite 201
Mississauga, Ontario
Canada L4V 1N3
Tel: 905 612 1016
Vitamins, supplements, herbal products, sports nutrition, natural
cosmetics. Locations across Canada

Allergy Asthma Information Association
20 South Road
Doaktown, New Brunswick
Canada E0C 1G0
Visit their website at http://www.sjfn.nb.ca

Canadian Cancer Society Information Service
No-Charge-Dial 1-888-939-3333
National Office:
10 Alcorn Road
Toronto, Ontario
Canada M4V 3B1
Tel: 416 961 7223

Canadian College of Naturopathic Medicine
2300 Yonge Street
Toronto, Ontario
Canada M4P 1E4
Tel: 416 486 8584
Email: info@www.ccnm.edu

Author's
acknowledgements

Lots of people have been generous with their time and encouragement
since I first took over writing What's the alternative? for *The Sunday Times*. They
include my sister Melissa Clark, Jeremy Langmead, Vera Taggart, and Michelle
Pamment of *The Sunday Times*, Tony Pinkus of Ainsworths pharmacy; the skin
psychologist Helen Sher; Dr. Charles Innes, Max Tomlinson, Cally Law, Abby Selby,
Anthony and Bharti Haynes, John Deacon, Fildelma Silsbury, Teresa Chris, and
Lorraine Turner. Thank you too to the Nutri Centre and Revital for assisting with a
reference library second to none and to Sophie Collins for thinking of me.